The Ecstasy of Rita Joe

George
Ryga's
The
Ecstasy
of
Rita
Joe

copyright © 1970 George Ryga

published with assistance from the Canada Council

Talonbooks
201 1019 East Cordova
Vancouver
British Columbia V6A 1M8
Canada

This book was typeset by Linda Gilbert of B.C. Monthly Typesetting Service, designed by David Robinson and printed by Hemlock Printers for Talonbooks.

Tenth printing: December 1976

The cover photograph was taken by Mac & Diane Parry.

Talonplays are edited by Peter Hay.

Rights to produce *The Ecstasy of Rita Joe*, in whole or in part, in any medium by any group, amateur or professional, are retained by the author and interested persons are requested to apply to him at Ryga & Associates, P.O. Box 430, Summerland, B.C. V0H 1Z0.

Canadian Shared Cataloguing in Publication Data
Ryga, George, 1932-
    George Ryga's The ecstasy of Rita
Joe
    ISBN 0-88922-000-X

    I. Title: The ecstasy of Rita Joe.
PS8585.Y393E29   C812'.5'4
PR9199.3.R

Preface

The play — *The Ecstasy of Rita Joe* — carries a message all Canada should hear. It is a message Canada needs to hear. I was amazed at the reaction the play received in Ottawa. People came to us to say that now, for the first time, they understood a little of what the Native Peoples have suffered and are suffering.

The Indian people at this very time need to put their message before Canada because laws are being readied that will affect the Indian for years to come. They need, above all, to create sympathy and understanding, for they are depressed economically. It is useless for people to hear if they do not listen with their hearts. *Rita Joe* helps them to listen with their hearts — and when hearts are open, ears can hear.

The message of *Rita Joe* is true — this I wish to make clear. The manner in which the author got his message across is another thing. I am not surprised that some people were hurt by the general condemnation of all organizations which have dealt with the Indian people. It would be wrong to infer that all were conniving . . . the play seems to suggest this. This, of course, is not true. Many, many good people I have known have worked hard and sincerely for our welfare.

But the message is true . . . of this there is no doubt and it should be heard by all.

Chief Dan George
Burrard Tribe, British Columbia

Introduction

The average life of even a successful play is three or four years. Many of them barely last a season. The handful that survive from any age or even from any one language become classics. It is a process as long and more infrequent than canonization.

The Ecstasy of Rita Joe was written and first produced during Canada's centennial. Since then it has received numerous productions, professional and amateur, large and small. It has been played in a French version by Gratien Gélinas. As a ballet, the Royal Winnipeg Ballet has toured Canada, the U.S. and Australia with it. During its U.S. premiere in Washington, D.C. in May, 1973, the play made a deep impression on audiences and critics alike, perhaps made more poignant by events at Alcatraz and Wounded Knee. And lastly, though on a note of special pride, the printed text by Talonbooks has gone through nine reprints since early 1970 for a total of 24,000 copies sold, excluding this present edition. In addition, a collection of three Ryga plays including *Rita Joe* from New Press in Toronto has also sold an equal number of copies.

A decade is not sufficient to pronounce a play a classic, but it is enough time to assess its importance to the development of Canadian theatre as well as to its author. On both these counts, it would be difficult to overestimate the importance of *The Ecstasy of Rita Joe*.

In 1967, as most people will recall, a Canadian play was so much of a rarity in English Canada that most directors could conveniently ignore indigenous drama altogether. The fledgling Playhouse Theatre Company in Vancouver was considered something of an oddity among regional theatres when Malcolm Black and later Joy Coghill persistently (even when there were no centennials to celebrate) produced two original plays by British Columbia writers every season. Later this policy was discontinued and the Playhouse joined ranks with all the other regional theatres across the land which still cling to the belief that theatre is an import business and that it thrives exclusively on imitation. Those four brief years, however, from 1965 to 1969, sufficed to establish a strong base for the Canadian playwrights' movement that has been in full swing since 1971, as well as explode certain myths which had prevented that movement from blossoming long before.

Some of these myths — many of which persist despite the erosion of their factual basis or credibility — have held that Canadian plays do not exist, or if they do, they are not worthy of production in Canadian theatres, theatres that are subsidized by Canadian taxpayers; that, if somehow they do get produced, they invariably lose money and lose more than proven plays of American or European origin, that the best way of dealing with the problem (i.e. the absence of worthwhile Canadian plays) is to sit back and wait until local playwrights manage to make use of their idyllic neglect and isolation and finally start coming up with some work that is recognizable and therefore acceptable by established, foreign standards. The fact that several theatres and festivals now exist solely dedicated to the productions of dozens and dozens of new Canadian plays every season has a great deal to do with the Vancouver Playhouse which back in those years broke all attendance records with the plays of Eric Nicol and George Ryga.

But there was something particularly new about *The Ecstasy of Rita Joe* and this has to do with the way George Ryga regards the theatre. It was the first time that a playwright had used the Vancouver Playhouse to confront its largely middle-class clientele with the reality of Skid Row blocks away. Ryga pointed a finger accusing that audience, the finger is still pointed in each and every play of his, even though since 1970 the Board of Directors have seen to it that those plays would not be produced at the Playhouse anymore.

Indian protest, Indian land claims and Indian rights are often featured by the media these days. As little as ten years ago, there was hardly a whisper. Indians themselves were only just waking up from a century and a half of oppression. Some of them were awake to take on roles in *The Ecstasy of Rita Joe*. Others woke up while watching it. The play did not focus on any particular issue so much as on the whole problem — white man's denial of the Indian's humanity. One aspect of the denial was the distorted image of the Indian as the exotic, happy or unhappy savage in white man's art and literature. It was only nine years before *Rita Joe* that Lister Sinclair's dramatization of Indian legends, *The World of the Wonderful Dark*, celebrated another centennial — white actors painted Indian in white man's version of Indian customs. Since *Rita Joe* that can never be done again, the nine years could have been a century.

For George Ryga, the play was just a beginning. He came to the theatre via poetry, the novel, radio and television dramas. Not in content, nor in style, nor in form have the half-dozen plays he has written in as many years resembled the standard fare in our subsidized theatres. He has little time for the import business or even for the classics; comparison is a luxury when one is empty-handed. The creation of a Canadian repertoire of classics is a near obsession with George Ryga. It is very late in the day, he believes, and time is running out. Despite the inroads made by Canadian playwrights in the past few years to force admission into their own theatres in their own country, Ryga, one of the best known dramatists in English Canada, cannot make even a minimal living from writing plays. And with each new work, he finds more doors closing rather than welcoming him. But as long as that is the case, he is at least fully assured that he must carry on, because he is on the right track.

Peter Hay
Fort Langley, B.C.
December, 1976

9

The Ecstasy of Rita Joe was commissioned and first produced by The Playhouse Theatre Centre, Vancouver, British Columbia. Premiere performance: November 23, 1967 at the Queen Elizabeth Playhouse, with the following cast:

Rita Joe	Frances Hyland
Jaimie Paul	August Schellenberg
Father, David Joe	Chief Dan George
Magistrate	Henry Ramer
Mr. Homer	Walter Marsh
Priest, Father Andrew	Robert Clothier
Eileen Joe	Patricia Gage
Old Indian Woman	Rae Brown
Teacher, Miss Donohue	Claudine Melgrave
Policeman	Bill Clarkson
Witness; Murderer	Merv Campone
Witness; Murderer	Alex Bruhanski
Witness	Jack Leaf
Murderer	Jack Buttrey
Young Indian Men	Leonard George, Robert Hall
	Frank Lewis, Paul Stanley
Guitarist	Willy Dunn
Singer	Ann Mortifee

Directed by George Bloomfield
Set and Lighting designed by Charles Evans
Costumes designed by Margaret Ryan
Music by Willy Dunn and Ann Mortifee
Lyrics by George Ryga
Stage Managed by Joel Miller
Choreography by Norbert Vesak

The Ecstasy of Rita Joe was re-mounted by The Playhouse Theatre Centre at the invitation of the Directors of the National Art Centre, for performance within the festival celebrating the opening of the National Art Centre in Ottawa, Ontario. First night: July 9, 1969 at the National Art Centre Theatre, with the following cast:

Rita Joe	Frances Hyland
Jaimie Paul	August Schellenberg
Father, David Joe	Chief Dan George
Magistrate	Alan Scarfe
Mr. Homer	Walter Marsh
Priest, Father Andrew	Robert Clothier
Eileen Joe	Patricia Gage
Old Indian Woman	Rae Brown
Teacher, Miss Donohue	Joy Coghill
Policeman	Jim McQueen
Witness: Murderer	Merv Campone
Witness: Murderer	Roger Dressler
Witness; Murderer	Al Kozlik
Young Indian Men	Leonard George, Robert Hall Frank Lewis, Paul Stanley
Guitarist-Singer	Ann Mortifee

Directed by David Gardner
Set and Lighting designed by Charles Evans
Costumes designed by Margaret Ryan
Music by Willy Dunn and Ann Mortifee
Lyrics by George Ryga
Stage Managed by Katherine Robertson
Choreography by Norbert Vesak

The Ecstasy of Rita Joe was translated into French by Gratien Gélinas and was produced by Foundation Nationale de la Comédie, Montréal, Québec. First night: November 19, 1969.

The Ecstasy of Rita Joe was first produced in the United States by Stephen Aaron, Producer, at The Washington Theatre Club, Washington, D.C. First night: May 2, 1973, with the following cast:

Rita Joe	Frances Hyland
Jamie Paul	Henry Bal
Father, David Joe	Chief Dan George
Magistrate	Roger DeKoven
Mr. Homer	Pat Corley
Priest, Father Andrew	Philip Baker Hall
Eileen Joe	Kathy Gittel
Old Indian Woman	Billie Lyon
Teacher, Miss Donohue	Laurinda Barrett
Policeman	John Jackson
Witness; Murderer	Richard DeAngelis
Witness; Murderer	Ronn Robinson
Murderer	Bruce MacDonald
Young Indian Men	Mike Halsey, John Tiger
Guitarist-Singer	Giulia Pagano
Music Ensemble	Dave Cole, Joel Eigen, Doug Shear

Directed by Harold Stone
Set designed by John H. Paull
Lighting designed by Michael Stauffer
Costumes designed by Danica Eskind
Music by Willy Dunn and Ann Mortifee
Lyrics by George Ryga
Stage Managed by E.O. Larson
Technical Direction by Keith Arnett

Act One

*A circular ramp beginning at floor level stage left
and continuing downward below floor level at
stage front, then rising and sweeping along stage
back at two-foot elevation to disappear in the
wings of stage left. This ramp dominates the
stage by wrapping the central and forward
playing area. A short approach ramp, meeting
with the main ramp at stage right, expedites
entrances from the wings of stage right.*

*The MAGISTRATE's chair and representation
of court desk are situated at stage right, enclosed
within the sweep of the ramp. At the foot of
the desk is a lip on stage right side. The SINGER
sits here, turned away from the focus of the
play. Her songs and accompaniment appear
almost accidental. She has all the reactions of
a white liberal folklorist with a limited concern
and understanding of an ethnic dilemma which
she touches in the course of her research and
work in compiling and writing folk songs. She
serves too as an alter ego to RITA JOE.*

*No curtain is used during the play. At the
opening, intermission and conclusion of the
play, the curtain remains up. The onus for
isolating scenes from the past and present in*

RITA JOE's life falls on highlight lighting.

*Backstage, there is a mountain cyclorama.
In front of the cyclorama there is a darker maze
curtain to suggest gloom and confusion, and a
cityscape.*

*The house lights and stage work lights remain
on. Backstage, cyclorama, and maze curtains are
up, revealing wall back of stage, exit doors, etc.*

*CAST, SINGER enter offstage singly and in
pairs from the wings, the exit doors at the back
of the theatre, and from the auditorium side
doors. The entrances are workmanlike and
untheatrical. When all the CAST is on stage,
they turn to face the audience momentarily.
The house lights dim.*

*The cyclorama is lowered into place. The
maze curtain follows. This creates a sense of
compression of stage into the auditorium.
Recorded voices are heard in a jumble of mutter-
ings and throat clearings. The MAGISTRATE
enters as the CLERK begins.*

CLERK: *recorded*
This court is in session. All present will rise . . .

The shuffling and scraping of furniture is heard.

*The CAST repeat "Rita Joe, Rita Joe." A
POLICEMAN brings on RITA JOE.*

MAGISTRATE:
Who is she? Can she speak English?

POLICEMAN:
Yes.

16

MAGISTRATE:
>Then let her speak for herself!

>*He speaks to the audience firmly and with*
>*reason.*

>To understand life in a given society, one must
>understand laws of that society. All relationships . . .

CLERK: *recorded*
>Man to man . . . man to woman . . . man to property
>. . . man to the state . . .

MAGISTRATE:
>. . . are determined and enriched by laws that have
>grown out of social realities. The quality of the law
>under which you live and function determines the
>real quality of the freedom that was yours today.

>*The rest of the CAST slowly move out.*

>Your home and your well-being were protected. The
>roads of the city are open to us. So are the galleries,
>libraries, the administrative and public buildings.
>There are buses, trains . . . going in and coming out.
>Nobody is a prisoner here.

RITA: *with humour, almost a sad sigh*
>The first time I tried to go home I was picked up by
>some men who gave me five dollars. An' then they
>arrested me.

>*The POLICEMAN retreats into the shadows.*
>*The SINGER crosses down.*

MAGISTRATE:
>Thousands leave and enter the city everyday . . .

RITA:
>It wasn't true what they said, but nobody'd believe
>me . . .

SINGER: *singing a recitivo searching for a melody*
Will the winds not blow
My words to her
Like the seeds
Of the dandelion?

MAGISTRATE: *smiles, as at a private joke*
Once . . . I saw a little girl in the Cariboo country.
It was summer then and she wore only a blouse
and skirt. I wondered what she wore in winter?

> *The MURDERERS hover in background on the
> upper ramp. One whistles and one lights a
> cigarette — an action which will be repeated at
> the end of the play.*

RITA: *moving to him, but hesitating*
You look like a good man. Tell them to let me go,
please!

> *The MAGISTRATE goes to his podium.*

MAGISTRATE:
Our nation is on an economic par with the state of
Arkansas . . . We are a developing country, but a
buoyant one. Still . . . the summer report of the
Economic Council of Canada predicts a reduction
in the gross national product unless we utilize our
manpower for greater efficiency. Employed, happy
people make for a prosperous, happy nation . . .

RITA: *exultantly*
I worked at some jobs, mister!

> *The MAGISTRATE turns to face RITA JOE.
> The MURDERERS have gone.*

MAGISTRATE:
Gainful employment. Obedience to the law . . .

RITA: *to the MATISTRATE*
Once I had a job . . .

> *He does not relate to her. She is troubled. She talks to the audience.*

Once I had a job in a tire store . . . an' I'd worry about what time my boss would come . . . He was always late . . . and so was everybody. Sometimes I got to thinkin' what would happen if he'd not come. And nobody else would come. And I'd be all day in this big room with no lights on an' the telephone ringing an' people asking for other people that weren't there . . . What would happen?

> *As she relates her concern, she laughs. Towards the end of her dialogue she is so amused by the absurdity of it all that she can hardly contain herself.*

> *Lights fade on the MAGISTRATE who broods in his chair as he examines his court papers.*

> *Lights up on JAIMIE PAUL approaching on the backstage ramp from stage left. He is jubilant, his laughter blending with her laughter. At the sound of his voice, RITA JOE runs to him, to the memory of him.*

JAIMIE:
I seen the city today and I seen things today I never knew was there, Rita Joe!

RITA: *happily*
I seen them too, Jaimie Paul!

> *He pauses above her, his mood light and childlike.*

JAIMIE:

I see a guy on top of a bridge, talkin' to himself . . .
an' lots of people on the beach watchin' harbour
seals . . . Kids feet popcorn to seagulls . . . an' I think
to myself . . . Boy! Pigeons eat pretty good here!

RITA:

In the morning, Jaimie Paul . . . very early in the
morning . . . the air is cold like at home . . .

JAIMIE:

Pretty soon I seen a little woman walkin' a big black
dog on a rope . . . Dog is mad . . . Dog wants a man!

*JAIMIE PAUL moves to RITA JOE. They
embrace.*

RITA:

Clouds are red over the city in the morning. Clara Hill
says to me if you're real happy . . . the clouds make
you forget you're not home . . .

*They laugh together. JAIMIE PAUL breaks
from her. He punctuates his story with wide,
sweeping gestures.*

JAIMIE:

I start singin' and some hotel windows open. I wave
to them, but nobody waves back! They're watchin'
me, like I was a harbour seal!

He laughs.

So I stopped singin'!

RITA:

I remember colours, but I've forgot faces already . . .

*JAIMIE PAUL looks at her as her mood changes.
Faint light on the MAGISTRATE brightens.*

20

A train whistle is white, with black lines . . . A sick
man talkin' is brown like an overcoat with pockets
torn an' string showin' . . . A sad woman is a room
with the curtains shut . . .

MAGISTRATE:
Rita Joe?

*She becomes sobered, but JAIMIE PAUL con-
tinues laughing. She nods to the MAGISTRATE,
then turns to JAIMIE PAUL.*

RITA:
Them bastards put me in jail. They're gonna do it
again, they said . . . Them bastards!

JAIMIE:
Guys who sell newspapers don't see nothin' . . .

RITA:
They drive by me, lookin' . . .

JAIMIE:
I'm gonna be a carpenter!

RITA:
I walk like a stick, tryin' to keep my ass from showin'
because I know what they're thinkin' . . . Them
bastards!

JAIMIE:
I got myself boots an' a new shirt . . . See!

RITA: *worried now*
I thought their jail was on fire . . . I thought it was
burning.

JAIMIE:
Room I got costs me seven bucks a week . . .

RITA:

I can't leave town. Everytime I try, they put me in
jail.

A POLICEMAN enters with a file folder.

JAIMIE:

They say it's a pretty good room for seven bucks a
week . . .

*JAIMIE PAUL begins to retreat backwards from
her, along the ramp to the wings of stage left.
She is isolated in a pool of light away from the
MAGISTRATE. The light isolation between her
and JAIMIE PAUL deepens, as the scene turns
into the courtroom again.*

MAGISTRATE:

Vagrancy . . . You are charged with vagrancy.

JAIMIE: *with enthusiasm, boyishly*

First hundred bucks I make, Rita Joe . . . I'm gonna
buy a car so I can take you everyplace!

RITA: *moving after him*

Jaimie!

*He retreats, dreamlike, into the wings. The spell
of memory between them is broken. Pools of
light between her and the MAGISTRATE
spread and fuse into a single light area. She
turns to the MAGISTRATE, worried and
confused.*

MAGISTRATE: *reading the documents in his hand*

The charge against you this morning is vagrancy . . .

*The MAGISTRATE continues studying the
papers he holds. She looks up at him and shakes
her head helplessly, then blurts out to him . . .*

22

RITA:
I had to spend last night in jail . . . Did you know?

MAGISTRATE:
Yes. You were arrested.

RITA:
I didn't know when morning came . . . There was no windows . . . The jail stinks! People in jail stink!

MAGISTRATE: *indulgently*
Are you surprised?

RITA:
I didn't know anybody there . . . People in jail stink like paper that's been in the rain too long. But a jail stinks worse. It stinks of rust . . . an' old hair . . .

The MAGISTRATE looks down at her for the first time.

MAGISTRATE:
You . . . are Rita Joe?

She nods quickly. A faint concern shows in his face. He watches her for a long moment.

I know your face . . . yet . . . it wasn't in this courtroom. Or was it?

RITA:
I don't know . . .

MAGISTRATE: *pondering*
Have you appeared before me in the past year?

RITA: *turning away from him, shrugging*
I don't know. I can't remember . . .

The MAGISTRATE throws his head back and laughs. The POLICEMAN joins in.

23

MAGISTRATE:
>You can't remember? Come now . . .

RITA: *laughing with him and looking to the POLICEMAN*
>I can't remember . . .

MAGISTRATE:
>Then I take it you haven't appeared before me. Certainly you and I would remember if you had.

RITA: *smiling*
>I don't remember . . .

>*The MAGISTRATE makes some hurried notes, but he is watching RITA JOE, formulating his next thought.*

>*She speaks naively . . .*

>My sister hitchhiked home an' she had no trouble like I . . .

MAGISTRATE:
>You'll need witnesses, Rita Joe. I'm only giving you eight hours to find witnesses for yourself . . .

RITA:
>Jaimie knows . . .

>*She turns to where JAIMIE PAUL had been, but the back of the stage is in darkness. The POLICEMAN exits suddenly.*

>Jaimie knew . . .

>*Her voice trails off pathetically. The MAGISTRATE shrugs and returns to studying his notes. RITA JOE chaffs during the silence which follows. She craves communion with people, with the MAGISTRATE.*

My sister was a dressmaker, mister! But she only worked two weeks in the city . . . An' then she got sick and went back to the reserve to help my father catch fish an' cut pulpwood.

She smiles.

She's not coming back . . . that's for sure!

MAGISTRATE: *with interest*
Should I know your sister? What was her name?

RITA:
Eileen Joe.

EILEEN JOE appears spotlit behind, a memory crowding in.

MAGISTRATE:
Eileen . . . that's a soft, undulating name.

RITA:
Two weeks, and not one white woman came to her to leave an order or old clothes for her to fix. No work at all for two weeks, an' her money ran out . . . Isn't that funny?

The MAGISTRATE again studies RITA JOE, his mind elsewhere.

MAGISTRATE:
Hmmmmm . . .

EILEEN JOE disappears.

RITA:
So she went back to the reserve to catch fish an' cut pulpwood!

MAGISTRATE:
I do know your face . . . Yes! And yet . . .

RITA:
Can I sit someplace?

MAGISTRATE: *excited*
I remember now . . . Yes! I was on holidays three
summers back in the Cariboo country . . . driving over
this road with not a house or field in sight . . . just
barren land, wild and windblown. And then I saw this
child beside the road, dressed in a blouse and skirt,
barefooted . . .

RITA: *looking around*
I don't feel so good, mister.

MAGISTRATE:
My God, she wasn't more than three or four years
old . . . walking towards me beside the road. When
I'd passed her, I stopped my car and then turned
around and drove back to where I'd seen her, for I
wondered what she could possibly be doing in such
a lonely country at that age without her father or
mother walking with her . . . Yet when I got back to
where I'd seen her, she had disappeared. She was
nowhere to be seen. Yet the land was flat for over
a mile in every direction . . . I had to see her. But
I couldn't . . .

He stares down at RITA JOE for a long moment.

You see, what I was going to say was that this child
had your face! Isn't that strange?

RITA: *with disinterest*
Sure, if you think so, mister . . .

MAGISTRATE:
Could she have been . . . your daughter?

RITA:
What difference does it make?

26

MAGISTRATE:
>Children cannot be left like that . . . It takes money
to raise children in the woods as in the cities . . .
There are institutions and people with more money
than you who could . . .

RITA:
>Nobody would get my child, mister!

>*She is distracted by EILEEN JOE's voice in her
memory. EILEEN's voice begins in darkness,
but as she speaks, a spotlight isolates her in
front of the ramp, stage left. EILEEN is on her
hands and knees, two buckets beside her. She
is picking berries in mime.*

EILEEN:
>First was the strawberries an' then the blueberries.
After the frost . . . we picked the cranberries . . .

>*She laughs with delight.*

RITA: *pleading with the MAGISTRATE, but her attention
on EILEEN* Let me go, mister . . .

MAGISTRATE:
>I can't let you go. I don't think that would be of any
use in the circumstances. Would you like a lawyer?

>*Even as he speaks, RITA JOE has entered the
scene with EILEEN picking berries.*

>*The MAGISTRATE's light fades on his podium.*

RITA:
>You ate the strawberries an' blueberries because you
were always a hungry kid!

EILEEN:
>But not cranberries! They made my stomach hurt.

> *RITA JOE goes down on her knees with*
> *EILEEN.*

RITA:
Let me pick . . . You rest.

> *She holds out the bucket to EILEEN.*

Mine's full aready . . . Let's change. You rest . . .

> *During the exchange of buckets, EILEEN*
> *notices her hands are larger than RITA JOE's.*
> *She is both delighted and surprised by this.*

EILEEN:
My hands are bigger than yours, Rita . . . Look!

> *She takes RITA JOE's hands in hers.*

When did my hands grow so big?

RITA: *wisely and sadly*
You've worked so hard . . . I'm older than you,
Leenie . . . I will always be older.

> *The two sisters are thoughtful for a moment,*
> *each watching the other in silence. Then RITA*
> *JOE becomes animated and resumes her mime*
> *of picking berries in the woods.*

We picked lots of wild berries when we were kids,
Leenie!

> *They turn away from their work and lie down*
> *alongside each other, facing the front of the*
> *stage.*

> *The light on them becomes summery, warm.*

In the summer, it was hot an' flies hummed so loud
you'd go to sleep if you sat down an' just listened.

EILEEN:

> The leaves on the poplars used to turn black an' curl
> together with the heat . . .

RITA:

> One day you and I were pickin' blueberries and a big
> storm came . . .

> *A sudden crash of thunder and a lightning
> flash. The lights turn cold and blue. The three
> MURDERERS stand in silhouette on a riser
> behind them. EILEEN cringes in fear, afraid
> of the storm, aware of the presence of the
> MURDERERS behind them.*

> *RITA JOE springs to her feet, her being attuned
> to the wildness of the atmosphere. Lightning
> continues to flash and flicker.*

EILEEN:

> Oh, no!

RITA: *shouting*

> It got cold and the rain an' hail came . . . the sky
> falling!

EILEEN: *crying in fear*

> Rita!

RITA: *laughing, shouting*

> Stay there!

> *A high flash of lightning, silhouetting the
> MURDERERS harshly. They take a step
> forward on the lightning flash. EILEEN dashes
> into arms of RITA JOE. She screams and
> drags RITA JOE down with her.*

> *RITA JOE struggles against EILEEN.*

RITA:

Let me go! What in hell's wrong with you? Let me go!

MAGISTRATE:

I can't let you go.

The lightning dies, but the thunder rumbles off into the distance. EILEEN subsides and pressing herself into the arms of RITA JOE as a small child to her mother, she sobs quietly.

RITA:

There, there . . .

With infinite tenderness.

You said to me, "What would happen if the storm hurt us an' we can't find our way home, but are lost together so far away in the bush?"

EILEEN looks up, brushing away her tears and smiling at RITA JOE.

RITA & EILEEN: *in unison*
Would you be my mother then?

RITA:

Would I be your mother?

RITA JOE releases EILEEN who looks back fearfully to where the MURDERERS had stood. They are gone. She rises and, collecting the buckets, moves hesitantly to where they had been. Confident now, she laughs softly and nervously to herself and leaves the stage.

RITA JOE rises and talks to EILEEN as she departs.

We walked home through the mud an' icy puddles among the trees. At first you cried, Leenie . . . and then you wanted to sleep. But I held you up an' when we got home you said you were sure you would've died in the bush if it hadn't been for us being together like that.

> *EILEEN disappears from the stage. The MAGISTRATE's light comes up. RITA JOE shakes her head sadly at the memory, then comes forward to the apron of the stage. She is proud of her sister and her next speech reveals this pride.*

She made a blouse for me that I wore everyday for one year, an' it never ripped at the armpits like the blouse I buy in the store does the first time I stretch . . .

> *She stretches languidly.*

I like to stretch when I'm happy! It makes all the happiness go through me like warm water . . .

> *The PRIEST, the TEACHER, and a YOUNG INDIAN MAN cross the stage directly behind her. The PRIEST wears a Roman collar and a check bush-jacket of a worker-priest. He pauses before passing RITA JOE and goes to meet her.*

PRIEST:

Rita Joe? When did you get back? How's life?

> *RITA JOE shrugs noncommittally.*

RITA:

You know me, Father Andrew . . . Could be better, could be worse . . .

PRIEST:

Are you still working?

RITA JOE is still noncommittal. She smiles at him. Her gestures are not definite.

RITA:
    I live.

PRIEST: *serious and concerned*
    It's not easy, is it?

RITA:
    Not always.

The TEACHER and the YOUNG INDIAN MAN exit.

PRIEST:
    A lot of things are different in the city. It's easier here on the reserve . . . Life is simpler. You can be yourself. That's important to remember.

RITA:
    Yes, Father . . .

The PRIEST wants to ask and say more, but he cannot. An awkward moment between them and he reaches out to touch her shoulder gently.

PRIEST:
    Well . . . be a good girl, Rita Joe . . .

RITA: *without turning after him*
    Goodbye, Father.

MAGISTRATE: *more insistently*
    Do you want a lawyer?

The PRIEST leaves stage right. As he leaves, cross light to where a happy JAIMIE PAUL enters from stage left. JAIMIE PAUL comes down to join RITA JOE.

JAIMIE:

This guy asked me how much education I got, an'
I says to him, "Grade six. How much education a
man need for such a job?" . . . An' the bum, he says
it's not enough! I should take night school. But I
got the job, an' I start next Friday . . . Like this . . .

*JAIMIE PAUL does a mock sweeping routine
as if he was cleaning a vast office building. He
and RITA JOE are both laughing.*

Pretty good, eh?

RITA:

Pretty good.

JAIMIE:

Cleaning the floors an' desks in the building . . .
But it's a government job, and that's good for life.
Work hard, then the government give me a raise . . .
I never had a job like that before . . .

RITA:

When I sleep happy, I dream of blueberries an'
sun an' all the nice things when I was a little kid,
Jaimie Paul.

*The sound of an airplane is heard. JAIMIE
PAUL looks up. RITA JOE also stares into the
sky of her memory. JAIMIE PAUL's face is
touched with pain and recollection. The
TEACHER, RITA JOE's FATHER, an OLD
WOMAN, four YOUNG INDIAN MEN and
EILEEN JOE come into the background quietly,
as if at a wharf watching the airplane leave the
village. They stand looking up until the noise
of the aircraft begins to diminish.*

JAIMIE:

That airplane . . . a Cessna . . .

He continues watching the aircraft and turns,
following its flight path.

She said to me, maybe I never see you again, Jaimie
Paul.

There is a faint light on the MAGISTRATE in
his chair. He is thoughtful, looking down at
his hands.

MAGISTRATE:
Do you want a lawyer?

RITA: *to JAIMIE PAUL*
Who?

JAIMIE:
Your mother . . . I said to her, they'll fix you up
good in the hospital. Better than before . . . .It was a
Cessna that landed on the river an' took her away . . .
Maybe I never see you again, Jaimie, she says to me.
She knew she was gonna die, but I was a kid and so
were you . . . What the hell did we know? I'll never
forget . . .

JAIMIE PAUL joins the village group on the
upper level.

SINGER: *singing an indefinite melody developing into a*
square-dance tune
There was a man in a beat-up hat
Who runs a house in the middle of town,
An' round his stove-pipe chimney house
The magpies sat, just a-lookin' round.

The Indian village people remain in the back of
the stage, still watching the airplane which has
vanished.

JAIMIE PAUL, on his way, passes MR. HOMER,
a white citizen who has the hurried but fulfilled

34

appearance of the socially responsible man.
MR. HOMER comes to front of the stage beside
RITA JOE. He talks directly to the audience.

MR. HOMER:

Sure, we do a lot of things for our Indians here in
the city at the Centre . . . Bring 'em in from the cold
an' give them food . . . The rest . . . Well, the rest
kinda take care of itself.

> *RITA JOE lowers her head and looks away from*
> *him. MR. HOMER moves to her and places*
> *his hand on her shoulders possessively.*

When your mother got sick we flew her out . . . You
remember that, Rita Joe?

RITA: *nodding, looking down*
Yes, Mr. Homer . . . Thank you.

MR. HOMER:

And we sent her body back for the funeral . . . Right,
Rita Joe?

> *The people of the village leave except for the*
> *YOUNG INDIAN MEN who remain and mime*
> *drinking.*

And then sometimes a man drinks it up an' leaves his
wife an' kids and the poor dears come here for help.
We give them food an' a place to sleep . . . Right, Rita?

RITA:
Yes.

MR. HOMER:

Clothes too . . . White people leave clothes here for
the Indians to take if they need 'em. Used to have
them all up on racks over there . . . just like in a
store . . .

He points.

But now we got them all on a heap on a table in the basement.

He laughs and RITA JOE nods with him.

Indian people . . . 'specially the women . . . get more of a kick diggin' through stuff that's piled up like that . . .

MR. HOMER chuckles and shakes his head.

There is a pale light on the MAGISTRATE, who is still looking down at his hands.

MAGISTRATE:
There are institutions to help you . . .

MR. HOMER again speaks to audience, but now he is angry over some personal beef.

MR. HOMER:
So you see, the Centre serves a need that's real for Indians who come to the city . . .

He wags his finger at the audience angrily.

It's the do-gooders burn my ass, you know! They come in from television or the newspaper . . . hang around just long enough to see a drunken Indain . . . an' bingo!

JAIMIE:
Bingo!

MR. HOMER:
That's their story! Next thing, they're seeing some kind of Red Power . . .

*The YOUNG INDIAN MEN laugh and RITA
JOE gets up to join them.*

. . . or beatin' the government over the head! Let
them live an' work among the Indians for a few
months . . . then they'd know what it's really like . . .

The music comes up sharply.

SINGER:

Round and round the cenotaph,
The clumsy seagulls play.
Fed by funny men with hats
Who watch them night and day.

*The four YOUNG INDIAN MEN join with
RITA JOE and dance. Leading the group is
JAIMIE PAUL. He is drunk, disheveled.*

*Light spreads before them as they advance
onstage. They are laughing rowdily.*

RITA JOE moves to them.

RITA:

Jaimie Paul?

*MR. HOMER leaves. JAIMIE PAUL is overtaken
by two of his companions who take him by the
arms, but he pushes them roughly away.*

JAIMIE:

Get the hell outa my way! . . . I'm as good a man as
him any time . . .

*JAIMIE PAUL crosses downstage to confront
a member of the audience.*

You know me? . . . You think I'm a dirty Indian, eh?
Get outa my way!

He puts his hands over his head and continues staggering away.

Goddamnit, I wanna sleep . . .

The YOUNG INDIAN MEN and JAIMIE PAUL exit. RITA JOE follows after JAIMIE PAUL, reaching out to touch him, but the SINGER stands in her way and drives her back, singing . . .

Music up tempo and volume.

SINGER:
    Oh, can't you see that train roll on,
    Its hot black wheels keep comin' on?
    A Kamloops Indian died today.
    Train didn't hit him, he just fell.
    Busy train with wheels on fire!

The music dies. A POLICEMAN enters.

POLICEMAN:
    Rita Joe!

He repeats her name many times.

The TEACHER enters ringing the school handbell and crosses through.

TEACHER: *calling*
    Rita Joe! Rita Joe! Didn't you hear the bell ring?
    The class is waiting . . . The class is always waiting
    for you.

The TEACHER exits.

MAGISTRATE &
POLICEMAN: *sharply, in unison*
    Rita Joe!

The POLICEMAN grabs and shakes RITA JOE to snap her out of her reverie.

Light up on the MAGISTRATE who sits erect, with authority.

MAGISTRATE:
> I ask you for the last time, Rita Joe . . . Do you want a lawyer?

RITA: *defiantly*
> What for? . . . I can take care of myself.

MAGISTRATE:
> The charge against you this morning is prostitution. Why did you not return to your people as you said you would?

> *The light on the backstage dies. RITA JOE stands before the MAGISTRATE and the POLICEMAN. She is contained in a pool of light before them.*

RITA: *nervous, with despair*
> I tried . . . I tried . . .

> *The MAGISTRATE settles back into his chair and takes a folder from his desk, which he opens and studies.*

MAGISTRATE:
> Special Constable Eric Wilson has submitted a statement to the effect that on June 18th he and Special Constable Schneider approached you on Fourth Avenue at nine-forty in the evening . . .

POLICEMAN:
> We were impersonating two deck-hands newly arrived in the city . . .

MAGISTRATE:
>You were arrested an hour later on charges of
>prostitution.

>*The MAGISTRATE holds the folder threaten-
>ingly and looks down at her. RITA JOE is
>defiant.*

RITA:
>That's a goddamned lie!

MAGISTRATE: *sternly, gesturing to the POLICEMAN*
>This is a police statement. Surely you don't think a
>mistake was made?

RITA: *peering into the light above her, shuddering*
>Everything in this room is like ice . . . How can you
>stay alive working here? . . . I'm so hungry I want to
>throw up . . .

MAGISTRATE:
>You have heard the statement, Rita Joe . . . Do you
>deny it?

RITA:
>I was going home, trying to find the highway . . .
>I knew those two were cops the moment I saw them
>. . . I told them to go f . . . fly a kite! They got sore
>then an' started pushing me around . . .

MAGISTRATE: *patiently now, waving down the objections
>of the POLICEMAN* Go on.

RITA:
>They followed me around until a third cop drove up.
>An' then they arrested me.

MAGISTRATE:
>Arrested you . . . Nothing else?

RITA:

They stuffed five dollar bills in my pockets when they had me in the car . . . I ask you, mister, when are they gonna charge cops like that with contributing to . . .

POLICEMAN:

Your Worship . . .

MAGISTRATE: *irritably, indicating the folder on the table before him* Now it's your word against this! You need references . . . People who know you . . . who will come to court to substantiate what you say . . . today! That is the process of legal argument!

RITA:

Can I bum a cigarette someplace?

MAGISTRATE:

No. You can't smoke in court.

The POLICEMAN smiles and exits.

RITA:

Then give me a bed to sleep on, or is the sun gonna rise an' rise until it burns a hole in my head?

Guitar music cues softly in the background.

MAGISTRATE:

Tell me about the child.

RITA:

What child?

MAGISTRATE:

The little girl I once saw beside the road!

RITA:

I don't know any girl, mister! When do I eat? Why does an Indian wait even when he's there first thing in the morning?

The pool of light tightens around MAGISTRATE and RITA JOE.

MAGISTRATE:

I have children . . . two sons . . .

RITA: *nodding*
Sure. That's good.

The MAGISTRATE gropes for words to express a message that is very precious to him.

MAGISTRATE:

My sons can go in any direction they wish . . . Into trades or university . . . But if I had a daughter, I would be more concerned . . .

RITA:

What's so special about a girl?

MAGISTRATE:

I would wish . . . Well, I'd be concerned about her choices . . . Her choices of living, school . . . friends . . . These things don't come as lightly for a girl. For boys it is different . . . But I would worry if I had a daughter . . . Don't hide your child! Someone else can be found to raise her if you can't!

RITA JOE shakes her head, a strange smile on her face.

Why not? There are people who would love to take care of it.

RITA:
> Nobody would get my child . . . I would sooner kill
> it an' bury it first! I am not a kind woman, mister
> judge!

MAGISTRATE: *at a loss*
> I see . . .

RITA: *a cry*
> I want to go home . . .

> > *Quick up tempo music is heard. Suddenly, the
> > lights change.*

> > *JAIMIE PAUL and the YOUNG INDIAN MEN
> > sweep over the backstage ramp, the light widen-
> > ing for them. RITA JOE moves into this railway
> > station crowd. She turns from one man to
> > another until she sees JAIMIE PAUL.*

> > *EILEEN JOE and an OLD WOMAN enter.*

RITA:
> Jaimie!

EILEEN: *happily, running to him*
> Jaimie Paul! God's sakes . . . When did you get back
> from the north? . . . I thought you said you wasn't
> coming until breakup . . .

> > *JAIMIE PAUL turns to EILEEN.*

JAIMIE:
> I was comin' home on the train . . . had a bit to drink
> and was feeling pretty good . . . Lots of women
> sleeping in their seats on the train . . . I'd lift their
> hats an' say, "Excuse me, lady . . . I'm lookin' for
> a wife!"

> > *He turns to the OLD WOMAN.*

One fat lady got mad, an' I says to her, "That's alright, lady . . . You got no worries . . . You keep sleepin'!"

Laughter.

JAIMIE PAUL and the OLD WOMAN move away.

EILEEN sees RITA JOE who is standing watching.

EILEEN:
   Rita! . . . Tom an' I broke up . . . Did I tell you?

RITA:
   No, Leenie . . . You didn't tell me!

EILEEN:
   He was no good . . . He stopped comin' to see me when he said he would. I kept waiting, but he didn't come . . .

RITA:
   I sent you a pillow for your wedding!

EILEEN:
   I gave it away . . . I gave it to Clara Hill.

RITA: *laughing bawdily and miming pregnancy*
   Clara Hill don't need no pillow now!

JAIMIE: *smiling, crossing by her and exiting*
   I always came to see you, Rita Joe . . .

RITA JOE looks bewildered.

OLD WOMAN: *exiting*
   I made two Saskatoon pies, Rita . . . You said next time you came home you wanted Saskatoon pie with lots of sugar . . .

44

EILEEN and the OLD WOMAN drift away.

JAIMIE PAUL moves on to the shadows.

The THREE MURDERERS enter in silhouette; one whistles. RITA JOE rushes to the YOUNG INDIAN MEN in stagefront.

RITA:

This is me, Rita Joe, God's sakes . . . We went to the same school together . . . Don't you know me now, Johnny? You remember how tough you was when you was a boy? . . . We tied you up in the Rainbow Creek and forgot you was there after recess . . . An' after school was out, somebody remembered . . .

She laughs.

And you was blue when we got to you. Your clothes was wet to the chin, an' you said, "That's a pretty good knot . . . I almost give up trying to untie it!"

The music continues. RITA JOE steps among the YOUNG INDIAN MEN and they mime being piled in a car at a drive-in.

Steve Laporte? . . . You remember us goin' to the drive-in and the cold rain comin' down the car windows so we couldn't see the picture show anyhow?

She sits beside STEVE LAPORTE. They mime the windshield wipers.

A cold white light comes up on playing area directly in front of the MAGISTRATE's chair. A MALE WITNESS of disheveled, dirty appearance steps into light and delivers testimony in a whining, defensive voice. He is one of the MURDERERS, but apart from the other three, he is nervous.

45

WITNESS:

I gave her three bucks . . . an' once I got her goin'
she started yellin' like hell! Called me a dog, pig . . .
some filthy kind of animal . . . So I slapped her
around a bit . . . Guys said she was a funny kind of
bim . . . would do it for them standing up, but not
for me she wouldn't . . . So I slapped her around . . .

The MAGISTRATE nods and makes a notation.
The light on the WITNESS dies.

RITA JOE speaks with urgency and growing
fear to STEVE LAPORTE.

RITA:

Then you shut the wipers off an' we were just sitting
there, not knowing what to do . . . I wish . . . we
could go back again there an' start livin' from that
day on . . . Jaimie!

RITA JOE looks at STEVE LAPORTE as at
a stranger. She stands and draws away from
him. JAIMIE PAUL enters behind RITA JOE.

There is a cold light before the MAGISTRATE
again and another MALE WITNESS moves into
the light, replacing the first WITNESS. He too
is one of the MURDERERS.

This WITNESS testifies with full gusto.

WITNESS:

Gave her a job in my tire store . . . took her over to
my place after work once . . . She was scared when I
tried a trick, but I'm easy on broads that get scared,
providin' they keep their voices down . . . After
that, I slipped her a fiver . . . Well, sir, she took the
money, then she stood in front of the window,
her head high an' her naked shoulders shakin' like she
was cold. Well, sir, she cried a little an' then she says,
"Goddamnit, but I wish I was a school teacher . . ."

He laughs and everyone onstage joins in the laughter.

The light dies out on the WITNESS. JAIMIE PAUL enters and crosses to RITA JOE. They lie down and embrace.

RITA:

You always came to see me, Jaimie Paul . . . The night we were in the cemetery . . . You remember, Jaimie Paul? I turned my face from yours until I saw the ground . . . an' I knew that below us . . . they were like us once, and now they lie below the ground, their eyes gone, the bones showin' . . . They must've spoke and touched each other here . . . like you're touching me, Jaimie Paul . . . an' now there was nothing over them, except us . . . an' wind in the grass an' a barbwire fence creaking. An' behind that, a hundred acres of barley.

JAIMIE PAUL stands.

That's something to remember, when you're lovin', eh?

The sound of a train whistle is heard. JAIMIE PAUL goes and the lights onstage fade.

The music comes up and the SINGER SINGS. As JAIMIE PAUL passes her, the SINGER pursues him up the ramp, and RITA JOE runs after them.

SINGER:

Oh, can't you see that train roll on,
Gonna kill a man, before it's gone?
Jaimie Paul fell and died.
He had it comin', so it's alright.
Silver train with wheels on fire!

The music dies instantly. RITA JOE's words come on the heels of music as a bitter extension of song.

She stands before the MAGISTRATE, again in the court, but looks back to where JAIMIE PAUL had been in the gloom. The POLICEMAN enters where JAIMIE PAUL has exited, replacing him, for the fourth trial scene.

RITA:

Jaimie, why am I here? . . . Is it . . . because people are talkin' about me and all them men . . . Is that why? I never wanted to cut cordwood for a living . . .

With great bitterness.

Never once I thought . . . it'd be like this . . .

MAGISTRATE:

What are we going to do about you, Rita Joe? This is the seventh charge against you in one year . . . Laws are not made to be violated in this way . . . Why did you steal?

RITA:

I was hungry. I had no money.

MAGISTRATE:

Yet you must have known you would be caught?

RITA:

Yes.

MAGISTRATE:

Are you not afraid of what is happening to you?

RITA:

I am afraid of a lot of things. Put me in jail. I don't care . . .

48

MAGISTRATE: *with forced authority*
>Law is a procedure. The procedure must be respected. It took hundreds of years to develop this process of law.

RITA:
>I stole a sweater . . . They caught me in five minutes!

>*She smiles whimsically at this. The MAGISTRATE is leafing through the documents before him. The POLICEMAN stands to one side of him.*

MAGISTRATE:
>The prosecutor's office has submitted some of the past history of Rita Joe . . .

POLICEMAN:
>She was born and raised on a reservation. Then came a brief period in a public school off the reservation . . . at which time Rita Joe established herself as something of a disruptive influence . . .

RITA:
>What's that mean?

MAGISTRATE: *turning to her, smiling*
>A trouble maker!

>*RITA JOE becomes animated, aware of the trap around her closing even at moments such as this.*

RITA:
>Maybe it was about the horse, huh? . . .

>*She looks up at the MAGISTRATE who is still smiling, offering her no help.*

>There was this accident with a horse . . . It happened like this . . . I was riding a horse to school an' some of the boys shot a rifle an' my horse bucked an' I fell off. I fell in the bush an' got scratched . . . The boys

caught the horse by the school and tried to ride him, but the horse bucked an' pinned a boy against a tree, breaking his leg in two places . . .

She indicates the place the leg got broken.

They said . . . an' he said I'd rode the horse over him on purpose!

MAGISTRATE:
Well . . . Did you?

RITA:
It wasn't that way at all, I tell you! They lied!

The POLICEMAN and the SINGER laugh.

MAGISTRATE:
Why should they lie, and Rita Joe alone tell the truth? . . . Or are you a child enough to believe the civilization of which we are a part . . .

He indicates the audience as inclusive of civilization from his point of view.

. . . does not understand Rita Joe?

RITA:
I don't know what you're saying.

MAGISTRATE: *with a touch of compassion*
Look at you, woman! Each time you come before me you are older. The lines in your face are those of . . .

RITA:
I'm tired an' I want to eat, mister! I haven't had grub since day before yesterday . . . This room is like a boat on water . . . I'm so dizzy . . . What the hell kind of place is this won't let me go lie down on grass?

50

She doubles over to choke back her nausea.

MAGISTRATE:
This is not the reservation, Rita Joe. This is another place, another time . . .

RITA: *straining to remember, to herself*
I was once in Whitecourt, Alberta. The cops are fatter there than here. I had to get out of Whitecourt, Alberta . . .

MAGISTRATE:
Don't blame the police, Rita Joe! The obstacles to your life are here . . .

He touches his forefinger to his temples.

. . . in your thoughts . . . possibly even in your culture . . .

RITA JOE turns away from him, searching the darkness behind her.

What's the matter?

RITA:
I want to go home!

MAGISTRATE:
But you can't go now. You've broken a law for which you will have to pay a fine or go to prison . . .

RITA:
I have no money.

MAGISTRATE: *with exasperation*
Rita Joe . . . It is against the law to solicit men on the street. You have to wash . . .

RITA JOE begins to move away from him, crossing the front of the stage along the apron, her walk cocky.

The light spreads and follows her.

You can't walk around in old clothes and running shoes made of canvas . . . You have to have some money in your pockets and an address where you live. You should fix your hair . . . perhaps even change your name. And try to tame that accent that sounds like you have a mouthful of sawdust . . . There is no peace in being extraordinary!

The light dies on the MAGISTRATE and the POLICEMAN.

RITA JOE is transported into another memory. JAIMIE PAUL enters and slides along the floor, left of centre stage. He is drunk, counting the fingers on his outstretched hands.

MR. HOMER has entered with a wagon carrying hot soup and mugs. Four YOUNG INDIAN MEN come in out of the cold. MR. HOMER speaks to audience in a matter-of-fact informative way.

MR. HOMER: *dispensing soup to the YOUNG INDIAN MEN* The do-gooders make something special of the Indian . . . There's nothing special here . . . At the centre here the quick cure is a bowl of stew under the belt and a good night's sleep.

JAIMIE:
Hey, Mister Homer! How come I got so many fingers? Heh?

He laughs.

MR. HOMER ignores JAIMIE PAUL and continues talking to the audience.

MR. HOMER:
>   I wouldn't say they were brothers or sisters to me . . .
>   No sir! But if you're . . .

>   *JAIMIE PAUL gets up and embraces RITA JOE.*

JAIMIE:
>   I got two hands an' one neck . . . I can kill more than
>   I can eat . . . If I had more fingers I would need
>   mittens big as pie plates . . . Yeh?

MR. HOMER: *to JAIMIE PAUL*
>   Lie down, Jaimie Paul, an' have some more sleep.
>   When you feel better, I'll get you some soup.

>   *RITA JOE laughs. JAIMIE PAUL weaves his
>   way uncertainly to where MR. HOMER stands.*

JAIMIE: *laughing*
>   I spit in your soup! You know what I say? . . . I say
>   I spit in your soup, Mister Homer . . .

>   *He comes to MR. HOMER and seems about to
>   do just what he threatens.*

MR. HOMER: *pushing him away with good humour*
>   I'll spit in your eyeball if you don't shut up!

JAIMIE: *breaking away from MR. HOMER, taunting*
>   You . . . are not Mister Homer!

MR. HOMER:
>   I'm not what?

JAIMIE:
>   You're not Mister Homer . . . You're somebody
>   wearing his pants an' shirt . . .

>   *He stumbles away.*

But you're not Mister Homer . . . Mister Homer never
gets mad . . . No sir, not Mister Homer!

MR. HOMER:
> I'm not mad . . . What're you talkin' about?

> > *JAIMIE PAUL turns and approaches the YOUNG
> > INDIAN MEN. He threatens to fall off the apron
> > of the stage.*

JAIMIE:
> No . . . not Mister Homer! An' I got ten fingers . . .
> How's that?

MR. HOMER:
> For Chris' sake, Jaimie . . . Go to sleep.

> > *JAIMIE PAUL stops and scowls, then grins
> > knowingly. He begins to mime a clumsy paddler
> > paddling a boat.*

JAIMIE: *laughing again*
> I know you . . . Hey? I know you! . . . I seen you up
> Rainbow Creek one time . . . I seen you paddling!

> *He breaks up with laughter.*

MR. HOMER: *amused, tolerant*
> Oh, come on . . . I've never been to Rainbow Creek.

> *JAIMIE PAUL controls his laughter.*

JAIMIE:
> Sure you been to Rainbow Creek . . .

> *He begins to mime paddling again.*

Next time you need a good paddler, you see me. I
have a govermen' job, but screw that. I'm gonna
paddle! I seen you paddle . . .

*Again he breaks up in laughter as he once more
demonstrates the quality of paddling he once
saw.*

*RITA JOE is fully enjoying the spectacle. So are
the YOUNG INDIAN MEN. MR. HOMER is
also amused by the absurdity of the situation.
JAIMIE PAUL turns, but chokes up with
laughter after saying . . .*

I have seen some paddlers . . . but you!

*JAIMIE PAUL turns and waves his hand
derisively, laughing.*

MR. HOMER:
It must've been somebody else . . . I've never been
to Rainbow Creek.

JAIMIE:
Like hell, you say!

*JAIMIE PAUL paddles the soup wagon out.
Guitar music comes in with an upbeat tempo.
RITA JOE and the YOUNG INDIAN MEN
dance to the beat. The YOUNG INDIAN MEN
then drift after MR. HOMER.*

*The light fades slowly on centre stage and the
music changes.*

*RITA JOE, happy in her memory, does a circling
butch walk in the fading light to the song of
the SINGER. At the conclusion of the song, she
is on the apron, stage right, in a wash of light
that includes the MAGISTRATE and the SINGER.*

SINGER:

> I woke up at six o'clock
> Stumbled out of bed,
> Crash of cans an' diesel trucks
> Damned near killed me dead.
>
> Sleepless hours, heavy nights,
> Dream your dreams so pretty.
> God was gonna have a laugh
> An' gave me a job in the city!

> *RITA JOE is still elated at her memory of
> JAIMIE PAUL and his story. With unusual
> candour, she turns girlishly before the
> MAGISTRATE, and in mild imitation of her
> own moment of drunkenness, begins telling him
> a story.*

> *Faint guitar music in the background continues.*

RITA:

> One night I drank a little bit of wine, an' I was outside
> lookin' at the stars . . . thinking . . . when I was a little
> girl how much bigger the trees were . . . no clouds, but
> suddenly there was a light that made the whole sky
> look like day . . .

> *Guitar out.*

> . . . just for a moment . . . an' before I got used to the
> night . . . I saw animals, moving across the sky . . .
> two white horses . . . A man was takin' them by the
> halters, and I knew the man was my grandfather . . .

> *She stares at the MAGISTRATE, unsure of
> herself now.*

MAGISTRATE:

> Yes! Is that all?

RITA:

> No . . . But I never seen my grandfather alive, and I
> got so sad thinkin' about it I wanted to cry. I wasn't
> sure it was him, even . . .

> *She begins to laugh.*

> I went an' telephoned the police and asked for the
> chief, but the chief was home and a guy asks what
> I want.

MAGISTRATE: *mildly amused*

> You . . . called the police?

RITA:

> I told the guy I'd seen God, and he says, "Yeh?
> What would you like us to do about it?" An' I said,
> "Pray! Laugh! Shout!"

MAGISTRATE:

> Go on . . .

RITA:

> He . . . asked where I'd seen God, an' I told him in
> the sky. He says you better call this number . . . It's
> the Air Force. They'll take care of it!

> *She laughs and the MAGISTRATE smiles.*

> I called the number the guy gave me, but it was
> nighttime and there was no answer! If God was
> to come at night, after office hours, then . . .

> *A terrible awkwardness sets in. There is a harsh
> light on her. She turns away, aware that she is
> in captivity.*

> *The MAGISTRATE stirs with discomfort.*

RITA: *with great fear*
How long will this be? Will I never be able to . . .

MAGISTRATE: *annoyed at himself, at her*
There is nothing here but a record of your convictions
. . . Nothing to speak for you and provide me with
any reason to moderate your sentence! What the hell
am I supposed to do? Violate the law myself because
I feel that somehow . . . I've known and felt . . . No!

He turns from her.

You give me no alternative . . . No alternative at all!

The MAGISTRATE packs up his books.

RITA:
I'll go home . . . jus' let me go home. I can't get out
of jail to find the highway . . . or some kind of job!

The MAGISTRATE stands.

MAGISTRATE:
Prison and fines are not the only thing . . . Have you,
for instance, considered that you might be an incurable
carrier? There are people like that . . . They cannot
come into contact with others without infecting
them. They cannot eat from dishes others may use
. . . They cannot prepare or touch food others will
eat . . . The same with clothes, cars, hospital beds!

The MAGISTRATE exits.

*RITA JOE shakes her head with disbelief. The
idea of perpetual condemnation is beyond her
comprehension. She falls to the floor.*

Guitar music is heard in the background.

*She turns away from the MAGISTRATE and the
light comes up over the ramp at the back of
the stage.*

*Another light comes up on centre stage left.
Here, EILEEN JOE and the OLD WOMAN are
miming clothes washing using a scrubbing
board and placing the wash into woven baskets.
The women and the girl are on their knees,
facing each other.*

*On the ramp above them, JAIMIE PAUL is
struggling with a POLICEMAN who is scolding
him softly for being drunk, abusive and noisy.
JAIMIE PAUL is jocular; the POLICEMAN,
harassed and worried. They slowly cross the
ramp from stage left.*

SINGER:
>Four o'clock in the morning,
>The sailor rides the ship
>An' I ride the wind!
>
>Eight o'clock in the morning,
>My honey's scoldin' the sleepyheads
>An' I'm scoldin' him.

JAIMIE: *to the POLICEMAN*
>On the Smoky River . . . four o'clock in the morning
>. . . Hey? There was nobody . . . just me . . . You
>know that?

POLICEMAN:
>No, I don't. Come on. Let's get you home.

>*JAIMIE PAUL moves forward and embraces the
>POLICEMAN.*

JAIMIE:
>You wanna see something?

JAIMIE PAUL takes out a coin to do a trick.

OLD WOMAN: *to EILEEN*
Your father's been very sick.

EILEEN:
He won't eat nothing . . .

OLD WOMAN:
Jus' sits and worries . . . That's no good.

JAIMIE PAUL finishes his coin trick.

JAIMIE:
You like that one? Hey, we both work for the govern-ment, eh?

They exit laughing.

Watch the rough stuff . . . Just don't make me mad.

OLD WOMAN:
If Rita Joe was to come and see him . . . maybe say good bye to him . . .

RITA: *calling from her world to the world of her strongest fears*   But he's not dying! I saw him not so long ago . . .

The women in her memory do not hear her. They continue discussing her father.

OLD WOMAN:
He loved her an' always worried . . .

RITA:
I didn't know he was sick!

OLD WOMAN:
You were smart to come back, Eileen Joe.

RITA: *again calling over the distance of her soul*
   Nobody told me!

SINGER:
   Nine o'clock in the evening,
   Moon is high in the blueberry sky
   An' I'm lovin' you.

JAIMIE: *now passing along the apron beside RITA JOE,*
   talking to the POLICEMAN You seen where I live?
   Big house with a mongolia in front . . . Fancy place!
   You wanna see the room I got?

POLICEMAN: *gruffly, aware that JAIMIE PAUL can*
   become angry quickly When I get holidays, we'll
   take a tour of everything you've got . . . but I don't
   get holidays until September!

   From the apron they cross to the stage rear
   diagonally, between the OLD WOMAN with
   EILEEN, and RITA JOE.

JAIMIE:
   You're a good man . . . Good for a laugh. I'm a good
   man . . . You know me!

POLICEMAN:
   Sure, you're first class when you're sober!

JAIMIE:
   I got a cousin in the city. He got his wife a stove an'
   washing machine! He's a good man . . . You know
   my cousin maybe?

   Fading off.

   They leave the stage.

   The OLD WOMAN has risen from her knees and
   wearily collected one basket of clothes. She
   climbs the ramp and moves to the wings, stage

right. EILEEN is thoughtful and slower, but she
also prepares her clothes wash and follows.

OLD WOMAN:
Nothing in the city I can see . . . only if you're lucky.
A good man who don't drink or play cards . . .
that's all.

EILEEN:
And if he's bad?

OLD WOMAN:
Then leave him. I'm older than you, Eileen . . . I
know what's best.

> *The OLD WOMAN exits. The guitar music dies*
> *out. JAIMIE PAUL's laughter and voice is heard*
> *offstage.*

JAIMIE: *offstage, loud, boisterous*
We both work for the gov'ment! We're buddies, no?
. . . You think we're both the same?

> *Laughter.*

> *The lights on the ramp and centre stage die.*

RITA: *following JAIMIE PAUL's laughter*
Good or bad, what difference? So long as he's a livin'
man!

> *RITA JOE and EILEEN giggle.*

> *The light spreads around her into pale infinity.*

> *The TEACHER enters on the ramp. She rings a*
> *handbell and stops a short distance from wings*
> *to peer around. She is a shy, inadequate woman*
> *who moves and behaves jerkily, the product of*
> *incomplete education and poor job placement.*

TEACHER: *in a scolding voice*
Rita! Rita Joe!

> *The bell rings.*

The class is waiting for you. The class is always waiting.

> *RITA JOE is startled to hear the bell and see the woman. She comes to her feet, now a child before the TEACHER, and runs to join EILEEN. JAIMIE PAUL and the YOUNG INDIAN MEN have entered with the bell and sit cross-legged on the floor as school children.*

RITA:
The sun is in my skin, Miss Donohue. The leaves is red and orange, and the wind stopped blowin' an hour ago.

> *The TEACHER has stopped to listen to this. RITA JOE and EILEEN, late again, slip into class and sit on the floor with the others.*

TEACHER:
Rita! What is a noun?

> *No answer. The kids poke RITA JOE to stand up.*

Did you hear what I asked?

RITA: *uncertain*
No . . . Yes?

TEACHER:
There's a lot you don't know . . . That kind of behaviour is exhibitionism! We are a melting pot!

RITA:
A melting pot?

TEACHER:
>A melting pot! Do you know what a melting pot is?

RITA:
>It's . . .

>*She shrugs.*

>. . . a melting pot!

>*The class laughs.*

TEACHER:
>Precisely! You put copper and tin into a melting pot and out comes bronze . . . It's the same with people!

RITA:
>Yes, Miss Donohue . . . out comes bronze . . .

>*Laughter again.*

>*The TEACHER calls RITA JOE over to her. The light fades on the other children.*

TEACHER:
>Rita, what was it I said to you this morning?

RITA:
>You said . . . wash my neck, clean my fingernails . . .

TEACHER: *cagey*
>No, it wasn't Rita!

RITA:
>I can't remember. It was long ago.

TEACHER:
>Try to remember, Rita.

RITA:

> I don't remember, Miss Donohue! I was thinkin'
> about you last night, thinkin' if you knew some . . .

TEACHER:

> You are straying off the topic! Never stray off the
> topic!

RITA:

> It was a dream, but now I'm scared, Miss Donohue.
> I've been a long time moving about . . . trying to find
> something! . . . I must've lost . . .

TEACHER:

> No, Rita. That is not important.

RITA:

> Not important?

TEACHER:

> No, Rita . . . Now you repeat after me like I said or
> I'm going to have to pass you by again. Say after me . . .

RITA:

> Sure. Say after you . . .

TEACHER:

> Say after me . . . "A book of verse underneath the
> spreading bough . . ."

RITA:

> "A book of verse underneath the spreading bough . . ."

TEACHER:

> "A jug of wine, a loaf of bread and thou beside me . . .
> singing in the wilderness."

RITA: *the child spell broken, she laughs bawdily*

> Jaimie said, "To heck with the wine an' loaf . . . Let's
> have some more of this here thou!"

Her laughter dies. She wipes her lips, as if trying to erase some stain there.

TEACHER: *peevish*
Alright, Rita . . . Alright, let's have none of that!

RITA: *plaintively*
I'm sorry, Miss Donohue . . . I'm sure sorry!

TEACHER:
That's alright.

RITA:
I'm sorry!

TEACHER:
Alright . . .

RITA:
Sorry . . .

TEACHER:
You will never make bronze! Coming from nowhere and going no place! Who am I to change that?

RITA JOE grips the edge of the desk with both hands, holding on tightly.

RITA:
No! They said for me to stay here, to learn something!

TEACHER: *with exasperation*
I tried to teach you, but your head was in the clouds, and as for your body . . . Well! I wouldn't even think what I know you do!

The TEACHER crosses amongst the other children.

RITA:

> I'm sorry . . . please! Let me say it after you again . . .
>
> *Blurting it out . . .*
>
> "A book of verse underneath the spreading . . ."

TEACHER:

> Arguing . . . always trying to upset me . . . and in grade four . . . I saw it then . . . pawing the ground for men like a bitch in heat!

RITA: *dismayed*
> It . . . isn't so!

TEACHER:

> You think I don't know? I'm not blind . . . I can see out of the windows.
>
> *The TEACHER marches off into wings and the class runs after her leaving RITA JOE alone onstage.*

RITA:

> That's a lie! For God's sake, tell the judge I have a good character . . . I am clean an' honest . . . Everything you said is right, I'm never gonna argue again . . . I believe in God . . . an' I'm from the country and lost like hell! Tell him!
>
> *She shakes her head sadly, knowing the extent of her betrayal.*
>
> They only give me eight hours to find somebody who knows me . . . An' seven and a half hours is gone already!
>
> *The lights on the scene dies.*

SINGER: *recitivo*
>> Things that were . . .
>> Life that might have been . . .

>> *A pale backlight on the back of the ramp comes*
>> *up.*

>> *Recorded sounds of crickets and the distant*
>> *sound of a train whistle are heard.*

>> *RITA JOE's FATHER and JAIMIE PAUL enter*
>> *on the ramp from stage left. The FATHER leads*
>> *the way. JAIMIE PAUL is behind, rolling a*
>> *cigarette. They walk slowly, thoughtfully,*
>> *following the ramp across and downstage.*
>> *RITA JOE stands separate, watching.*

>> The blue evening of the first
>> Warm day
>> Is the last evening.
>> There'll not be another
>> Like it.

JAIMIE:
>> No more handouts, David Joe . . . We can pick an' can
>> the berries ourselves.

FATHER:
>> We need money to start a cooperative like that.

JAIMIE:
>> Then some other way!

>> *The old man listens, standing still, to the sounds*
>> *of the train and night.*

FATHER:
>> You're a young man, Jaimie Paul . . . young an' angry.
>> It's not good to be that angry.

JAIMIE:

> We're gonna work an' live like people . . . Not be afraid
> all the time . . . Stop listening to an old priest an'
> Indian department guys who're working for a pension!

FATHER:

> You're young man, Jaimie Paul . . .

JAIMIE:

> I say stop listening, David Joe! . . . In the city they
> never learned my name. It was "Hey, fella" . . . or
> "You, boy" . . . That kind of stuff.

> *Pause. The sound of the train whistle is heard.*

FATHER:

> A beautiful night, Jaimie Paul.

JAIMIE:

> We can make some money. The berries are good this
> year!

> *JAIMIE PAUL is restless, edgy, particularly on
> the train whistle sound.*

FATHER:

> Sometimes . . . children . . . You remember everyday
> with them . . . Never forget you are alive with children .

> *JAIMIE PAUL turns away and begins to retrace
> his steps.*

JAIMIE:

> You want us all to leave an' go to the city? Is that
> what you want?

> *The FATHER shakes his head. He does not wish
> for this, but the generation spread between them
> is great now. JAIMIE PAUL walks away with a
> gesture of contempt.*

The sounds die.

*The light dies and isolates the FATHER and
RITA JOE.*

RITA:

You were sick, an' now you're well.

FATHER: *in measured speech, turning away from RITA
JOE, as if carefully recalling something of great
importance* You left your father, Rita Joe . . . never
wrote Eileen a letter that time . . . Your father was
pretty sick man that time . . . pretty sick man . . .
June ninth he got the cold, an' on June twenty he . . .

RITA:

But you're alive! I had such crazy dreams I'd wake up
laughing at myself!

FATHER:

I have dreams too . . .

*RITA JOE moves forward to him. She stops
talking to him, as if communicating thoughts
rather than words. He remains standing where he
is, facing away from her.*

RITA:

I was in a big city . . . so many streets I'd get lost like
nothin' . . . When you got sick I was on a job . . .

FATHER:

June ninth I got the cold . . .

RITA:

Good job in a tire store . . . Jaimie Paul's got a job
with the government, you know?

FATHER:

Pretty sick man, that time . . .

70

RITA:

A good job in a tire store. They was gonna teach me how to file statements after I learned the telephone. Bus ticket home was twenty dollars . . . But I got drunk all the same when I heard an' I went in and tried to work that day . . .

She smiles and shakes her head.

Boy, I tried to work! Some day that was!

FATHER:

I have dreams . . . Sometimes I'm scared . . .

They finally look at each other.

RITA: *shuddering*
I'm so cold . . .

FATHER:

Long dreams . . . I dream about Rita Joe . . .

Sadly.

Have to get better. I've lived longer, but I know nothing . . . Nothing at all. Only the old stories.

RITA JOE moves sideways to him. She is smiling happily.

RITA:

When I was little, a man came out of the bush to see you. Tell me why again!

The FATHER hesitates, shaking his head, but he is also smiling.

The light of their separate yearnings fades out and the front of the stage is lit with the two of them together.

The FATHER turns and comes forward to meet her.

FATHER:
You don't want to hear that story again.

He sits on the slight elevation of the stage apron. RITA JOE sits down in front of him and snuggles between his knees. He leans forward over her.

RITA:
It's the best story I ever heard!

FATHER:
You were a little girl . . . four years old already . . . an' Eileen was getting big inside your mother. One day it was hot . . . sure was hot. Too hot to try an' fish in the lake, because the fish was down deep where the water was cold.

RITA:
The dog started to bark . . .

FATHER:
The dog started to bark . . . How!

FATHER & RITA: *in unison*
How! How! How!

FATHER:
Barking to beat hell an' I says to myself why . . . on such a hot day? Then I see the bushes moving . . . somebody was coming to see us. Your mother said from inside the house, "What's the matter with that dog?" An' I says to her, "Somebody coming to see me." It was big Sandy Collins, who ran the sawmill back of the reserve. Business was bad for big Sandy then . . . but he comes out of that bush like he was being chased . . . his clothes all wet an' stickin' to him . . . his cap in his hands, an' his face black with the heat and dirt from hard work . . . He says to me,

72

"My little Millie got a cough last night an' today
she's dead." . . . "She's dead," big Sandy says to me.
I says to him, "I'm sorry to hear that, Sandy . . .
Millie is the same age as my Rita." And he says to
me, "David Joe . . . Look, you got another kid
coming . . . Won't make much difference to you . . .
Sell me Rita Joe like she is for a thousand dollars!"

*RITA JOE giggles. The FATHER raises his hand
to silence her.*

"A thousand dollars is a lot of money, Sandy," I says
to him . . . "lots of money. You got to cut a lot of
timber for a thousand dollars." Then he says to me,
"Not a thousand cash at once, David Joe. First I
give you two-hundred-fifty dollars . . . When Rita
Joe comes ten years old and she's still alright, I give
you the next two-hundred-fifty . . . An' if she don't
die by fifteen, I guarantee you five-hundred dollars
cash at once!"

*RITA JOE and the FATHER break into laughter.
He reaches around her throat and draws her close.*

So you see, Rita Joe, you lose me one thousand dollars
from big Sandy Collins!

They continue laughing.

*A harsh light on the MAGISTRATE, who enters
and stands on his podium.*

MAGISTRATE:
Rita Joe, when was the last time you had dental
treatment?

*RITA JOE covers her ears, refusing to surrender
this moment of security in the arms of her
FATHER.*

RITA:
  I can't hear you!

MAGISTRATE: *loudly*
  You had your teeth fixed ever?

  RITA JOE comes to her feet and turns on him.

RITA:
  Leave me alone!

MAGISTRATE:
  Have you had your lungs x-rayed recently?

RITA:
  I was hungry, that's all!

MAGISTRATE: *becoming staccato, machine-like in his
    questions* When was your last Wasserman taken?

RITA:
  What's that?

  *RITA JOE hears the TEACHER's voice. She
  turns to see the approaching TEACHER give the
  MAGISTRATE testimony.*

  The stage is lit in a cold blue light now.

TEACHER: *crisply, to the MAGISTRATE as she approaches,
  her dialogue a reading* Dear Sir . . . In reply to your
  letter of the twelfth, I cannot in all sincerity provide
  a reference of good character for one Rita Joe . . .

  *The WITNESSES do not see her and the
  testimony takes on the air of a nightmare for
  RITA JOE. She is baffled and afraid. The
  TEACHER continues to quietly repeat her
  testimony.*

  RITA JOE appeals to the MAGISTRATE.

RITA:
> Why am I here? What've I done?

MAGISTRATE:
> You are charged with prostitution.

> *Her FATHER stands and crosses upstage to the*
> *ramp to observe. He is joined by EILEEN JOE,*
> *the OLD WOMAN and the PRIEST. MR. HOMER*
> *approaches briskly from stage left.*

MR. HOMER:
> She'd been drinking when she comes into the centre
> . . . Nothing wrong in that I could see, 'specially on
> a Friday night. So I give her some soup an' a sandwich.
> Then all of a sudden in the middle of a silly argument,
> she goes haywire . . . an' I see her comin' at me . . . I'll
> tell you, I was scared! I don't know Indian women
> that well!

MAGISTRATE:
> Assault!

> *RITA JOE retreats from him and the TEACHER*
> *and MR. HOMER now stand before the MAGIS-*
> *TRATE as if they were frozen. MR. HOMER*
> *repeats his testimony under the main dialogue.*
> *JAIMIE PAUL staggers in from stage right, over*
> *the ramp, heading to the wings of lower stage left.*

JAIMIE: *to himself*
> What the hell are they doing?

RITA: *running to him*
> Say a good word for me, Jaimie!

JAIMIE:
> They fired me yesterday . . . What the hell's the use
> of living?

JAIMIE PAUL leaves the stage as the SCHOOL BOARD CLERK enters to offer further testimony to the MAGISTRATE.

SCHOOL BOARD CLERK:
I recommended in a letter that she take school after grade five through correspondence courses from the Department of Education . . . but she never replied to the form letter the school division sent her . . .

RITA: *defending herself to the MAGISTRATE*
That drunken bastard Mahoney used it to light fire in his store . . . He'd never tell Indians when mail came for us!

SCHOOL BOARD CLERK:
I repeat . . . I wish our position understood most clearly . . . No reply was ever received in this office to the letter we sent to Rita Joe!

RITA:
One letter . . . one letter for a lifetime?

TEACHER:
Say after me! "I wandered lonely as a cloud, that floats on high o'er vales and hills . . . when all at once I saw a crowd . . . a melting pot . . ."

A POLICEMAN and a MALE WITNESS enter. The PRIEST crosses downstage. The testimonies are becoming a nightmare babble.

RITA JOE is stung, stumbles backward from all of them as they face the MAGISTRATE with their condemnations.

POLICEMAN:
We were impersonating two deckhands . . .

The PRIEST is passing by RITA JOE. He makes

76

the sign of the cross and offers comfort in a thin
voice, lost in the noise.

PRIEST:
>Be patient, Rita . . . The young are always stormy,
>but in time, your understanding will deepen . . .
>There is an end to all things.

WITNESS:
>I gave her a job, but she was kind of slow . . . I can't
>wait around, there's lots of white people goin' lookin'
>for work . . . so I figure, to hell with this noise . . .

MAGISTRATE: *loudly over the other voices*
>Have your ears ached?

RITA:
>No!

MAGISTRATE:
>Have you any boils on your back? Any discharge?
>When did you bathe last?

>*The MURDERERS appear and circle RITA JOE.*

>Answer me! Drunkenness! Shoplifting! Assault!
>Prostitution, prostitution, prostitution, prostitution!

RITA: *her voice shrill, cutting over the babble*
>I don't know what happened . . . but you got to listen
>to me and believe me, mister!

>*The babble ceases abruptly.*

>*Pleading with them as best she knows.*

>You got rules here that was made before I was born
>. . . I was hungry when I stole something . . . an' I
>was hollerin' I was so lonely when I started whoring . . .

>*The MURDERERS come closer.*

MAGISTRATE:
>Rita Joe . . . Has a doctor examined you? . . . I mean, really examined you? Rita Joe . . . You might be carrying and transmitting some disease and not aware of it!

RITA: *breaking away from the MURDERERS*
>Bastards!

>*To the MAGISTRATE.*

>Put me in jail . . . I don't care . . . I'll sign anything. I'm so goddamn hungry I'm sick . . . Whatever it is, I'm guilty!

>*She clutches her head and goes down in a squat of defeat.*

MAGISTRATE:
>Are you free of venereal disease?

RITA:
>I don't know. I'm not sick that way.

MAGISTRATE:
>How can you tell?

RITA: *lifting her face to him*
>I know . . . A woman knows them things . . .

>*Pause.*

MAGISTRATE:
>Thirty days!

>*The POLICEMAN leads RITA JOE off and the house lights come up.*

>*The ACTORS and the SINGER walk off the stage, leaving emptiness as at opening of the act.*

Act Two

The house lights dim.

A POLICEMAN brings RITA JOE in downstage centre. She curls up in her jail cell and sleeps.

RITA JOE's FATHER enters on the ramp and crosses down to the audience.

The stage work lights die down. Lights isolate RITA JOE's FATHER. Another light with prison bar shadows isolates RITA JOE in her area of the stage.

FATHER: *looking down on RITA JOE*
I see no way . . . no way . . . It's not clear like trees against snow . . . . not clear at all . . .

To the audience.

But when I was fifteen years old, I leave the reserve to work on a threshing crew. They pay a dollar a day for a good man . . . an' I was a good strong man. The first time I got work there was a girl about as old as I . . . She'd come out in the yard an' watch the men working at the threshing machine. She had eyes that were the biggest I ever seen . . . like fifty-cent pieces . . . an' there was always a flock of geese around her.

Whenever I see her I feel good. She used to stand an'
watch me, an' the geese made a helluva lot of noise.
One time I got off my rick an' went to get a drink of
water . . . but I walked close to where she was
watching me. She backed away, and then ran from
me with the geese chasin' after her, their wings out
an' their feet no longer touching the ground . . .
They were white geese . . . The last time Rita Joe
come home to see us . . . the last time she ever come
home . . . I watched her leave . . . and I seen geese
running after Rita Joe the same way . . . white geese
. . . with their wings out an' their feet no longer
touching the ground. And I remembered it all, an'
my heart got so heavy I wanted to cry . . .

The light fades to darkness on the FATHER, as
he exits up the ramp and off. RITA JOE wakes
from her dream, cold, shaking, desperate.

SINGER:
The blue evening of the
First warm day
Is the last evening.
There's not be another
Like it.

The PRIEST enters from darkness with the
POLICEMAN. He is dressed in a dark suit
which needs pressing. He stops in half shadow
outside RITA JOE's prison light.

The scene between them is played out in the
manner of two country people meeting in
a time of crisis. Their thoughts come slowly,
incompletely. There is both fear and helplessness
in both characters.

PRIEST:
I came twice before they'd let me see you . . .

RITA JOE jumps to her feet. She smiles at him.

RITA:

Oh, Father Andrew!

PRIEST:

Even so, I had to wait an hour.

A long pause.

He clumsily takes out package of cigarettes and matches from his pocket and hands them to her, aware that he is possibly breaking a prison regulation.

I'm sorry about this, Rita.

RITA JOE tears the package open greedily and lights a cigarette. She draws on it with animal satisfaction.

RITA:

I don't know what's happening, Father Andrew.

PRIEST:

They're not . . . hurting you here?

RITA:

No.

PRIEST:

I could make an appointment with the warden if there was something . . .

RITA:

What's it like outside? . . . Is it a nice day outside? . . . I heard it raining last night . . . Was it raining?

PRIEST:

It rains a lot here . . .

RITA:

When I was a kid, there was leaves an' a river . . .
Jaimie Paul told me once that maybe we never see
those things again.

*A long pause. The PRIEST struggles with
himself.*

PRIEST:

I've never been inside a jail before . . . They told me
there was a chapel . . .

He points indefinitely back.

RITA:

What's gonna happen to me? . . . That judge sure got
sore . . .

She laughs.

PRIEST: *with disgust, yet unsure of himself*
Prostitution this time?

RITA:

I guess so . . .

PRIEST:

You know how I feel . . . City is no place for you . . .
nor for me . . . I've spent my life in the same sur-
roundings as your father!

RITA:

Sure . . . but you had God on your side!

She smiles mischievously. The PRIEST angers.

PRIEST:

Rita, try to understand . . . Our Lord Jesus once met
a woman such as you beside the well . . . He forgave
her!

RITA:

I don't think God hears me here . . . Nobody hears me now, nobody except cops an' pimps an' bootleggers!

PRIEST:

I'm here. I was there when you were born.

RITA:

You've told me lots of times . . . I was thinkin' about my mother last night . . . She died young . . . I'm older than she was . . .

PRIEST:

You mother was a good, hard-working woman. She was happy . . .

A pause between them.

RITA:

There was frost on the street at five o'clock Tuesday morning when they arrested me . . . Last night, I remembered things flyin' an' kids runnin' past me trying to catch a chocolate wrapper that's blowin' in the wind . . .

She presses her hands against her bosom.

It hurts me here to think about them things!

PRIEST:

I worry about you . . . Your father worries too . . . I baptized you . . . I watched you and Leenie grow into women!

RITA:

Yes . . . I seen God in what you said . . . In your clothes! In your hair!

PRIEST:

But you're not the woman I expected you to be . . .
Your pride, Rita . . . your pride . . . may bar you
from heaven.

RITA: *mocking him*

They got rules there too . . . in heaven?

PRIEST: *angry*

Rita! . . . I'm not blind . . . I can see! I'm not deaf . . .
I know all about you! So does God!

RITA:

My uncle was Dan Joe . . . He was dyin' and he said
to me, "Long ago the white man come with Bibles
to talk to my people, who had the land. They talk for
hundred years . . . then we had all the Bibles, an' the
white man had our land . . ."

PRIEST:

Don't blame the Church! We are trying to help . . .

RITA: *with passion*

How? I'm looking for the door . . .

PRIEST: *tortured now*

I . . . will hear your confession . . .

RITA:

But I want to be free!

PRIEST: *stiffly*

We learn through suffering, Rita Joe . . . We will only
be free if we become humble again.

> *Pause.*

Will you confess, Rita Joe?

> *A long pause.*

I'm going back on the four o'clock bus.

He begins walking away into the gloom.

I'll tell your father I saw you, and you looked well.

He is suddenly relieved.

RITA: *after him as he leaves*
You go to hell!

The PRIEST turns sharply.

Go tell your God . . . when you see him . . . Tell him
about Rita Joe an' what they done to her! Tell him
about yourself too! . . . That you were not good
enough for me, but that didn't stop you tryin'!
Tell him that!

The PRIEST hurries away.

Guitar in. RITA JOE sits down, brooding.

SINGER:
I will give you the wind and a sense of wonder
As the child by the river, the reedy river.
I will give you the sky wounded by thunder
And a leaf on the river, the silver river.

*A light comes up on the ramp where JAIMIE
PAUL appears, smiling and waving to her.*

JAIMIE: *shouts*
Rita Joe! I'm gonna take you dancing after work
Friday . . . That job's gonna be alright!

RITA JOE springs to her feet, elated.

RITA:
Put me back in jail so I can be free on Friday!

A sudden burst of dance music. The stage lights up and JAIMIE PAUL approaches her. They dance together, remaining close in the front centre stage.

SINGER:
>Round an' round the cenotaph,
>The clumsy seagulls play.
>Fed by funny men with hats
>Who watch them night and day.
>
>Sleepless hours, heavy nights,
>Dream your dreams so pretty.
>God was gonna have a laugh
>An' gave me a job in the city!

>*The music continues for the interlude.*

>*Some YOUNG INDIAN MEN run onto the stage along the ramp and join JAIMIE PAUL and RITA JOE in their dance. The MURDERERS enter and elbow into the group, their attention specifically menacing towards JAIMIE PAUL and RITA JOE. A street brawl begins as a POLICEMAN passes through on his beat. The MURDERERS leave hastily.*

>I woke up at six o'clock,
>Stumbled out of bed.
>Crash of steel and diesel trucks
>Damned near killed me dead
>
>Sleepless hours, heavy nights,
>Dream your dreams so pretty.
>God was gonna have a laugh
>An' gave me a job in the city!

>*Musical interlude.*

>*RITA JOE and JAIMIE PAUL continue dancing languidly. The YOUNG INDIAN MEN exit.*

I've polished floors an' cut the trees,
Fished and stooked the wheat.
Now "Hallelujah, Praise the Lord,"
I sing before I eat!

Sleepless hours, heavy nights,
Dream your dreams so pretty.
God was gonna have a laugh
An' gave me a job in the city!

> *Musical interlude.*

> *The music dies as the YOUNG INDIAN MEN
> wheel in a brass bed, circle it around and exit.*

> *The stage darkens except for a pool of light
> where RITA JOE and JAIMIE PAUL stand,
> embracing. JAIMIE PAUL takes her hand
> and leads her away.*

JAIMIE:
> Come on, Rita Joe . . . you're slow.

RITA: *happy in her memories, not wishing to forget too soon,
> hesitating*   How much rent . . . for a place where you
> can keep babies?

JAMIE:
> I don't know . . . maybe eighty dollars a month.

RITA:
> That's a lot of money.

JAMIE:
> It costs a buck to go dancin' even . . .

> *They walk slowly along the apron to stage left,
> as if following a street to JAIMIE PAUL's rooming
> house.*

It's a good place . . . I got a sink in the room. Costs
seven bucks a week, that's all!

RITA:

That's good . . . I only got a bed in my place . . .

JAIMIE:

I seen Mickey an' Steve Laporte last night.

RITA:

How are they?

JAIMIE:

Good . . . We're goin' to a beer parlour Monday night
when I get paid . . . the same beer parlour they threw
Steve out of! Only now there's three of us goin' in!

They arrive at and enter his room.

*A spot illuminates the bed near the wings of
stage left. It is old, dilapidated.*

*JAIMIE PAUL and RITA JOE enter the area of
light around the bed. He is aware that the room
is more drab than he would wish it.*

How do you like it . . . I like it!

RITA: *examining room critically*
It's . . . smaller than my place.

JAIMIE:

Sit down.

*She sits on edge of the bed and falls backward
into a springless hollow.*

*He laughs nervously. He is awkward and confused.
The ease they shared walking to his place is now
constricted.*

88

I was gonna get some grub today, but I was busy . . .
Here . . .

> *He takes a chocolate bar out of his shirt pocket
> and offers it to her. She opens it, breaks off a
> small piece, and gives the remainder to him. He
> closes the wrapper and replaces the bar in his
> pocket. She eats ravenously. He walks around
> the bed nervously.*

No fat d.p.'s gonna throw me or the boys out of that
beer parlour or he's gonna get this!

> *He holds up a fist in a gesture that is both
> poignant and futile. She laughs and he glowers
> at her.*

I'm tellin' you!

RITA:
If they want to throw you out, they'll throw you out.

JAIMIE:
Well, this is one Indian guy they're not pushing around
no more!

RITA:
God helps them who help themselves.

JAIMIE:
That's right!

> *He laughs.*

I was lookin' at the white shirts in Eaton's and this
bugger comes an' says to me, you gonna buy or you
gonna look all day?

RITA: *looking around her*
It's a nice room for a guy, I guess . . .

JAIMIE:

It's a lousy room!

> *RITA JOE lies back lengthwise in the bed.*
> *JAIMIE PAUL sits on the bed beside her.*

RITA:

You need a good job to have babies in the city . . .
Clara Hill gave both her kids away they say . . .

JAIMIE:

Where do kids like that go?

RITA:

Foster homes, I guess.

JAIMIE:

If somebody don't like the kid, back they go to
another foster home?

RITA:

I guess so . . . Clara Hill don't know where her kids
are now.

> *JAIMIE PAUL twists sharply in his anger.*

JAIMIE:

Goddamn it!

RITA:

My father says . . .

> *JAIMIE PAUL rises, crosses round the bed to*
> *the other side.*

JAIMIE: *harshly*

I don't want to hear what your father got to say! He's
like . . . like the kind of Indian a white man likes!
He's gonna look wise and wait forever . . . For what?
For the kids they take away to come back?

90

RITA:

He's scared . . . I'm scared . . . We're all scared,
Jaimie Paul.

*JAIMIE PAUL lies face down and mimes a gun
through the bars.*

JAIMIE:

Sometimes I feel like takin' a gun and just . . .

*He waves his hand as if to liquidate his environ-
ment and all that bedevils him. He turns over on
his back and lies beside RITA JOE.*

I don't know . . . Goddamnit, I don't know what to
do. I get mad an' then I don't know what I'm doing
or thinkin' . . . I get scared sometimes, Rita Joe.

RITA: *tenderly*

We're scared . . . everybody . . .

JAIMIE:

I'm scared of dyin' . . . in the city. They don't care
for one another here . . . You got to be smart or have
a good job to live like that.

RITA:

Clara Hill's gonna have another baby . . .

JAIMIE:

I can't live like that . . . A man don't count for much
here . . . Women can do as much as a man . . . There's
no difference between men and women. I can't live
like that.

RITA:

You got to stop worrying, Jaimie Paul. You're gonna
get sick worryin'.

JAIMIE:

You can't live like that, can you?

91

RITA:
No.

JAIMIE:
I can't figure out what the hell they want from us!

RITA: *laughing*
Last time I was in trouble, the judge was asking me what I wanted from him! I could've told him, but I didn't!

They both laugh. JAIMIE PAUL becomes playful and happy.

JAIMIE:
Last night I seen television in a store window. I seen a guy on television showing this knife that cuts everything it's so sharp . . . He was cutting up good shoes like they were potatoes . . . That was sure funny to see!

Again they laugh in merriment at the idea of such a demonstration. JAIMIE PAUL continues with his story, gesturing with his hands.

Chop . . . chop . . . chop . . . A potful of shoes in no time! What's a guy gonna do with a potful of shoes? Cook them?

They continue laughing and lie together again. Then JAIMIE PAUL sobers. He rises from the bed and walks around it. He offers his hand to RITA JOE, who also rises.

Drily.

Come on. This is a lousy room!

SINGER: *reprise*
God was gonna have a laugh,
And gave me a job in the city!

92

*The light goes down on RITA JOE and JAIMIE
PAUL. The YOUNG INDIAN MEN clear the
bed.*

*Cross fade the rear ramp of the stage. RITA
JOE's FATHER and the PRIEST enter and cross
the stage.*

PRIEST:

She got out yesterday, but she wouldn't let me see
her. I stayed an extra day, but she wouldn't see me.

FATHER: *sadly*

I must go once more to the city . . . I must go to see
them.

PRIEST:

You're an old man . . . I wish I could persuade you
not to go.

FATHER:

You wouldn't say that if you had children, Andrew . . .

The lights go down on them.

*The lights come up on centre stage front. Three
YOUNG INDIAN MEN precede MR. HOMER,
carrying a table between them. MR. HOMER
follows with a hamper of clothes under his arm.*

MR. HOMER:

Yeh . . . right about there is fine, boys. Got to get the
clutter out of the basement . . . There's mice coming
in to beat hell.

*MR. HOMER empties the clothes hamper on the
table. The YOUNG INDIAN MEN step aside
and converse in an undertone.*

*On the ramp, a YOUNG INDIAN MAN weaves
his way from stage left and down to centre stage*

*where the others have brought the table. He is
followed by JAIMIE PAUL and RITA JOE, who
mime his intoxicated progress.*

MR. HOMER speaks to the audience . . .

The Society for Aid to the Indians sent a guy over to
see if I could recommend someone who'd been . . .
Well, through the mill, like they say . . . An' then
smartened up an' taken rehabilitation. The guy said
they just wanted a rehabilitated Indian to show up
at their annual dinner. No speeches or fancy stuff . . .
just be there.

*The YOUNG INDIAN MAN lies down carefully
to one side of MR. HOMER.*

Hi, Louie. Not that I would cross the street for the
Society . . . They're nothing but a pack of do-gooders
out to get their name in the papers . . .

*The YOUNG INDIAN MAN begins to sing a
tuneless song, trailing off into silence.*

Keep it down, eh, Louie? I couldn't think of anybody
to suggest to this guy . . . so he went away pretty
sore . . .

*RITA JOE begins to rummage through the
clothes on the table. She looks at sweaters and
holds a red one thoughtfully in her hands.*

*JAIMIE PAUL is in conversation with the
YOUNG INDIAN MEN to one side of the table.*

*MR. HOMER turns from audience to see RITA
JOE holding the sweater.*

Try it on, Rita Joe . . . That's what the stuff's there
for.

JAIMIE PAUL turns. He is in a provocative mood, seething with rebellion that makes the humour he triggers both biting and deceptively innocent. The YOUNG INDIAN MEN respond to him with strong laughter. JAIMIE PAUL takes a play punch at one of them.

JAIMIE:

Whoops! Scared you, eh?

He glances back at MR. HOMER, as if talking to him.

Can't take it, eh? The priest can't take it. Indian Department guys can't take it . . . Why listen to them? Listen to the radio if you want to hear something.

The YOUNG INDIAN MEN laugh.

Or listen to me! You think I'm smart?

YOUNG INDIAN MAN:

You're a smart man, Jaimie Paul.

JAIMIE:

Naw . . . I'm not smart . . .

He points to another YOUNG INDIAN MAN.

This guy here . . . calls himself squaw-humper . . . He's smart! . . . . Him . . . he buys extra big shirts . . . more cloth for the same money . . . That's smart!

Laughter.

I'm not smart.

Seriously.

You figure we can start a business an' be our own boss?

95

YOUNG INDIAN MAN:
> I don't know about that . . .

>> *JAIMIE PAUL leaves them and goes to lean over the YOUNG INDIAN MAN who is now asleep on the floor.*

JAIMIE:
> Buy a taxi . . . Be our own boss . . .

>> *He shakes the sleeping YOUNG INDIAN MAN, who immediately begins his tuneless song.*

> Aw, he's drunk . . .

>> *JAIMIE PAUL goes over to the table and stares at the YOUNG INDIAN MAN beyond the table.*

>> *Soberly.*

> Buy everything we need . . . Don't be bums! Bums need grub an' clothes . . . Bums is bad for the country, right Mr. Homer?

MR. HOMER: *nods*
> I guess so . . .

>> *To RITA JOE who is now wearing the old sweater.*

> Red looks good on you, Rita Joe . . . Take it!

>> *JAIMIE PAUL goes over and embraces RITA JOE, then pushes her gently away.*

JAIMIE:
> She looks better in yellow. I never seen a red dandelion before.

>> *He and the YOUNG INDIAN MEN laugh, but the laughter is hollow.*

MR. HOMER:

Come on, Jaimie! Leave the girl alone. That's what it's here for . . . Are you working?

JAIMIE: *evasive, needling*

Yeh! . . . No! . . . "Can you drive?" the guy says to me. "Sure, I can drive," I says to him. "Okay," he says, "then drive this broom until the warehouse is clean."

They all laugh.

MR. HOMER:

That's a good one . . . Jaimie, you're a card . . . Well, time to get some food for you lot . . .

MR. HOMER leaves. RITA JOE feels better about the sweater. She looks to one of the YOUNG INDIAN MEN for approval. JAIMIE PAUL becomes grim-faced.

RITA:

Do you like it?

YOUNG INDIAN MAN:

Sure. It's a nice sweater . . . Take it.

JAIMIE:

Take it where? Take it to hell . . . Be men!

He points after MR. HOMER.

He's got no kids . . . Guys like that get mean when they got no kids . . . We're his kids an' he means to keep it that way! Well, I'm a big boy now!

To RITA JOE.

I go to the employment office. I want work an' I want it now. "I'm not a goddamned cripple," I says to him. An' he says he can only take my name! If

work comes he'll call me! "What the hell is this,"
I says to him. "I'll never get work like that . . .
There's no telephone in the house where I got a
room!"

> *MR. HOMER returns pushing a wheeled tray
> on which he has some food for sandwiches, a
> loaf of bread and a large cutting knife. He begins
> to make some sandwiches.*

RITA: *scolding JAIMIE PAUL*
You won't get work talking that way, Jaimie Paul!

JAIMIE:
Why not? I'm not scared. He gets mad at me an' I say
to him . . . "You think I'm some stupid Indian you're
talkin' to? Heh? You think that?"

> *JAIMIE PAUL struts and swaggers to demonstrate
> how he faced his opponent at the employment
> office.*

MR. HOMER: *cutting bread*
You're a tough man to cross, Jaimie Paul.

JAIMIE: *ignoring MR. HOMER, to the YOUNG INDIAN
MEN* Boy, I showed that bastard who he was talkin'
to!

RITA:
Did you get the job?

JAIMIE: *turns to her, laughing boyishly*
No! He called the cops an' they threw me out!

> *They all laugh. The YOUNG INDIAN MEN go to
> the table now and rummage through the clothes.*

MR. HOMER:
Take whatever you want, boys . . . there's more clothes
comin' tomorrow.

98

*JAIMIE PAUL impulsively moves to the table
where the YOUNG INDIAN MEN are fingering
the clothes. He pushes them aside and shoves the
clothes in a heap leaving a small corner of table
clean. He takes out two coins from his pockets
and spits in his hands.*

JAIMIE:
> I got a new trick . . . Come on, Mister Homer . . . I'll
> show you! See this!

> *He shows the coins, then slams his hands palms
> down on the table.*

Which hand got the coins?

MR. HOMER:
> Why . . . one under each hand . . .

JAIMIE:
> Right!

> *He turns up his hands.*

Again?

> *He collects the coins and slaps his hands down
> again.*

Where are the coins now? Come on, guess!

> *MR. HOMER is confident now and points to
> right hand with his cutting knife. JAIMIE PAUL
> laughs and lifts his hands.*

> *The coins are under his left hand.*

MR. HOMER:
> Son of a gun.

JAIMIE:
> You're a smart man.

> *He puts coins in his pockets and laughing, turns to RITA JOE, who stands uncertainly dressed in the red sweater. She likes the garment, but she is aware JAIMIE PAUL might resent her taking it. The YOUNG INDIAN MEN again move to the table, and MR. HOMER returns to making sandwiches.*

MR. HOMER:
> There's a good pair of socks might come in handy for one of you guys!

> *A YOUNG INDIAN MAN pokes his thumbs through the holes in the socks, and laughs.*

JAIMIE:
> Sure . . . Take the socks! Take the table!

> *He slaps the table with his hands and laughs.*

> Take Mister Homer cutting bread! Take everything!

MR. HOMER:
> Hey, Jaimie!

JAIMIE:
> Why not? There's more comin' tomorrow, you said!

RITA:
> Jaimie!

MR. HOMER:
> You're sure in a smart-assed mood today, aren't you?

JAIMIE: *pointing to the YOUNG INDIAN MAN with the socks, but talking to MR. HOMER* Mister, friend Steve over there laughs lots . . . He figures . . . the way to get along an' live is to grab his guts an' laugh

100

at anything anybody says. You see him laughing all the time. A dog barks at him an' he laughs . . .

Laughter from the YOUNG INDIAN MAN.

Laughs at a fence post fallin' . . .

Laughter.

Kids with funny eyes make him go haywire . . .

Laughter.

Can of meat an' no can opener . . .

MR. HOMER watches the YOUNG INDIAN MEN and grins at JAIMIE PAUL.

MR. HOMER:
> Yeh . . . He laughs quite a bit . . .

JAIMIE:
> He laughs at a rusty nail . . . Nice guy . . . laughs all the time.

MR. HOMER: *to JAIMIE PAUL, holding the knife*
> You wanted mustard on your bread or just plain?

JAIMIE:
> I seen him cut his hand and start laughin' . . . Isn't that funny?

The YOUNG INDIAN MEN laugh, but with less humour now.

MR. HOMER: *to JAIMIE PAUL*
> You want mustard? . . . I'm talkin' to you!

JAIMIE:
> I'm not hungry.

*The YOUNG INDIAN MEN stop laughing
altogether. They become tense and suspicious
of JAIMIE PAUL, who is watching them severely.*

MR. HOMER:
Suit yourself. Rita?

*She shakes her head slowly, her gaze on JAIMIE
PAUL's face.*

RITA:
I'm not hungry.

*MR. HOMER looks from RITA JOE to JAIMIE
PAUL, then to the YOUNG INDIAN MEN. His
manner stiffens.*

MR. HOMER:
I see . . .

*JAIMIE PAUL and RITA JOE touch hands and
come forward to sit on the apron of the stage,
front. A pale light is on the two of them.*

*The stage lights behind them fade. A low light
that is diffused and shadowy remains on the
table where MR. HOMER has prepared the food.
The YOUNG INDIAN MEN move slowly to the
table and begin eating the sandwiches MR.
HOMER offers to them. The light on the table
fades very low.*

*JAIMIE PAUL hands a cigarette to RITA JOE
and they smoke.*

*Light comes up over the rear ramp. RITA JOE's
FATHER enters onto the ramp from the wings
of stage right. His step is resolute. The PRIEST
follows behind him a few paces. They have been
arguing. Both are dressed in work clothes of
heavy trousers and windbreakers.*

JAIMIE:
> When I'm laughing, I got friends.

RITA:
> I know, Jaimie Paul . . .

PRIEST:
> That was the way I found her, that was the way I left her.

JAIMIE: *bitterly*
> When I'm laughing, I'm a joker . . . A funny boy!

FATHER:
> If I was young . . . I wouldn't sleep. I would talk to people . . . let them all know!

JAIMIE:
> I'm not dangerous when I'm laughing . . .

PRIEST:
> You could lose the reserve and have nowhere to go!

FATHER:
> I have lost more than that! Young people die . . . young people don't believe me . . .

JAIMIE:
> That's alright . . . that's alright . . .

> *The light dies out on JAIMIE PAUL and RITA JOE. The light also dies out on MR. HOMER and YOUNG INDIAN MEN.*

PRIEST:
> You think they believe that hot-headed . . . that troublemaker?

FATHER: *turning to face the PRIEST*
> Jaimie Paul is a good boy!

PRIEST:

> David Joe . . . you and I have lived through a lot. We need peace now, and time to consider what to do next.

FATHER:

> Eileen said to me last night . . . she wants to go to the city. I worry all night . . . What can I do?

PRIEST:

> I'll talk to her, if you wish.

FATHER: *angry*

> And tell her what? . . . . Of the animals there . . .

> *He gestures to the audience.*

> Who sleep with sore stomachs because . . . they eat too much?

PRIEST:

> We mustn't lose the reserve and the old life, David Joe . . . Would you . . . give up being chief on the reserve?

FATHER:

> Yes!

PRIEST:

> To Jamie Paul?

FATHER:

> No . . . To someone who's been to school . . . Maybe university . . . who knows more.

PRIEST: *relieved by this, but not reassured*

> The people here need your wisdom and stability, David Joe. There is no man here who knows as much about hunting and fishing and guiding. You can survive . . . What does a youngster who's been away to school know of this?

FATHER: *sadly*
>If we only fish an' hunt an' cut pulpwood . . . pick strawberries in the bush . . . for a hundred years more, we are dead. I know this, here . . .

>*He touches his breast.*

>*The light dies on the ramp.*

>*A light rises on stage front, on JAIMIE PAUL and RITA JOE sitting at the apron of the stage. MR. HOMER is still cutting bread for sandwiches. The three YOUNG INDIAN MEN have eaten and appear restless to leave. The fourth YOUNG INDIAN MAN is still asleep on the floor.*

>*RITA JOE has taken off the red sweater, but continues to hold it in her hand.*

JAIMIE: *to MR. HOMER*
>One time I was on a trapline five days without grub. I ate snow an' I walked until I got back. You think you can take it like me?

>*MR. HOMER approaches JAIMIE PAUL and holds out a sandwich to him.*

MR. HOMER:
>Here . . . have a sandwich now.

>*JAIMIE PAUL ignores his hand.*

RITA:
>Mister Homer don't know what happened, Jaimie Paul.

>*MR. HOMER shrugs and walks away to his sandwich table.*

JAIMIE:
>Then he's got to learn . . . Sure he knows!

To MR. HOMER.

Sure he knows! He's feedin' sandwiches to Indian
bums . . . He knows. He's the worst kind!

*The YOUNG INDIAN MEN freeze and MR.
HOMER stops.*

MR. HOMER: *coldly*
I've never yet asked a man to leave this building.

*RITA JOE and JAIMIE PAUL rise to their feet.
RITA JOE goes to the clothes table and throws
the red sweater back on the pile of clothes.
JAIMIE PAUL laughs sardonically.*

To RITA JOE.

Hey, not you, girl . . . You take it!

She shakes her head and moves to leave.

RITA:
I think we better go, boys.

*The sleeping YOUNG INDIAN MAN slowly
raises his head, senses there is something wrong,
and is about to be helped up, when . . .*

JAIMIE:
After five days without grub, the first meal I threw
up . . . stomach couldn't take it . . . But after that
it was alright . . .

To MR. HOMER, with intensity.

I don't believe nobody . . . No priest nor government
. . . They don't know what it's like to . . . to want an'
not have . . . to stand in line an' nobody sees you!

MR. HOMER:

> If you want food, eat! You need clothes, take them.
> That's all . . . But I'm runnin' this centre my way, and
> I mean it!

JAIMIE:

> I come to say no to you . . . That's all . . . that's all!

> *He throws out his arms in a gesture that is both
> defiant and childlike. The gesture disarms some
> of MR. HOMER's growing hostility.*

MR. HOMER:

> You've got that right . . . No problems. There's others
> come through here day an' night . . . No problem.

JAIMIE:

> I don't want no others to come. I don't want them to
> eat here!

> *He indicates his friends.*

> If we got to take it from behind a store window, then
> we break the window an' wait for the cops. It's better
> than . . . than this!

> *He gestures with contempt at the food and the
> clothes on the table.*

MR. HOMER:

> Rita Joe . . . where'd you pick up this . . . this
> loudmouth anyway?

RITA: *slowly, firmly*

> I think . . . Jaimie Paul's . . . right.

> *MR. HOMER looks from face to face. The three
> YOUNG INDIAN MEN are passive, staring into
> the distance. The fourth is trying hard to clear
> his head. JAIMIE PAUL is cold, hostile. RITA
> JOE is determined.*

MR. HOMER: *decisively*
> Alright! You've eaten . . . looked over the clothes
> . . . Now clear out so others get a chance to come in!
> Move!

> *He tries to herd everyone out and the four*
> *YOUNG INDIAN MEN begin to move away.*
> *JAIMIE PAUL mimics the gestures of MR.*
> *HOMER and steps in front of the YOUNG*
> *INDIAN MEN herding them back in.*

JAIMIE:
> Run, boys, run! Or Mister Homer gonna beat us up!

> *RITA JOE takes JAIMIE PAUL's hand and tries*
> *to pull him away to leave.*

RITA:
> Jaimie Paul . . . you said to me no trouble!

> *JAIMIE PAUL pulls his hand free and jumps*
> *back of the clothes table. MR. HOMER comes*
> *for him, unknowingly still carrying the slicing*
> *knife in his hand. An absurd chase begins around*
> *the table. One of the YOUNG INDIAN MEN*
> *laughs, and stepping forward, catches hold of*
> *MR. HOMER's hand with the knife in it.*

YOUNG INDIAN MAN:
> Hey! Don't play with a knife, Mister Homer!

> *He gently takes the knife away from MR.*
> *HOMER and drops it on the food table behind.*
> *MR. HOMER looks at his hand, an expression*
> *of shock on his face.*

> *JAIMIE PAUL gives him no time to think about*
> *the knife and what it must have appeared like*
> *to the YOUNG INDIAN MEN. He pulls a large*
> *brassiere from the clothes table and mockingly*
> *holds it over his breasts, which he sticks out*

*enticingly at MR. HOMER. The YOUNG INDIAN
MEN laugh. MR. HOMER is exasperated and
furious. RITA JOE is frightened.*

RITA:
It's not funny, Jaimie!

JAIMIE:
It's funny as hell, Rita Joe. Even funnier this way!

*JAIMIE PAUL puts the brassiere over his head,
with the cups down over his ears and the straps
under his chin. The YOUNG INDIAN MEN are
all laughing now and moving close to the table.
MR. HOMER makes a futile attempt at driving
them off.*

*Suddenly JAIMIE PAUL's expression turns to
one of hatred. He throws the brassiere on the
table and gripping its edge, throws the table and
clothes over, scattering the clothes. He kicks at
them. The YOUNG INDIAN MEN all jump in
and, picking up the clothes, hurl them over
the ramp.*

*RITA JOE runs in to try and stop them. She
grips the table and tries lifting it up again.*

MR. HOMER: *to JAIMIE PAUL*
Cut that out, you sonofabitch!

*JAIMIE PAUL stands watching him. MR.
HOMER is in a fury. He sees RITA JOE
struggling to right the table. He moves to her
and pushes her hard.*

You slut! . . . You breed whore!

RITA JOE recoils.

With a shriek of frustration, she attacks MR.
HOMER, tearing at him. He backs away, then
turns and runs.

JAIMIE PAUL overturns the table again. The
others join in the melée with the clothes.

A POLICEMAN enters and grabs JAIMIE PAUL.
RITA JOE and the four YOUNG INDIAN MEN
exit, clearing away the tables and remaining
clothes.

A sharp, tiny spotlight comes up on the face
and upper torso of JAIMIE PAUL. He is wild
with rebellion as the POLICEMAN forces him,
in an arm lock, down towards the audience.

JAIMIE: *screaming defiance at the audience*
Not jus' a box of cornflakes! When I go in, I want the
whole store! That's right . . . the whole goddamned
store!

Another sharp light on the MAGISTRATE
standing on his podium looking down at JAIMIE
PAUL.

MAGISTRATE:
Thirty days!

JAIMIE: *held by POLICEMAN*
Sure, sure . . . Anything else you know?

MAGISTRATE:
Thirty days!

JAIMIE:
Gimme back my truth!

MAGISTRATE:
We'll get larger prisons and more police in every town
and city across the country!

110

JAIMIE:
>Teach me who I really am! You've taken that away!
>Give me back the real me so I can live like a man!

MAGISTRATE:
>There is room for dialogue. There is room for diagreement and there is room for social change . . . but within the framework of institutions and traditions in existence for that purpose!

JAIMIE: *spits*
>Go to hell! . . . I can die an' you got nothing to tell me!

MAGISTRATE: *in a cold fury*
>Thirty days! And after that, it will be six months! And after that . . . God help you!

>*The MAGISTRATE marches off his platform and offstage.*

>*JAIMIE PAUL is led off briskly in the other direction offstage.*

>*The lights change.*

>*RITA JOE enters, crossing the stage, exchanging a look with the SINGER.*

SINGER:
>Sleepless hours, heavy nights,
>Dream your dreams so pretty.
>God was gonna have a laugh
>An' gave me a job in the city!

>*RITA JOE walks the street. She is smoking a cigarette. She is dispirited.*

>*The light broadens across the stage.*

>*RITA JOE's FATHER and JAIMIE PAUL enter the stage from the wings of centre stage left.*

111

They walk slowly towards where RITA JOE stands.

At the sight of her FATHER, RITA JOE moans softly and hurriedly stamps out her cigarette. She visibly straightens and waits for the approaching men, her expression one of fear and joy.

FATHER:
I got a ride on Miller's truck . . . took me two days . . .

JAIMIE:
It's a long way, David Joe.

The FATHER stops a pace short of RITA JOE and looks at her with great tenderness and concern.

FATHER: *softly*
I come . . . to get Rita Joe.

RITA:
Oh . . . I don't know . . .

She looks to JAIMIE PAUL for help in deciding what to do, but he is sullen and uncommunicative.

FATHER:
I come to take Rita Joe home . . . We got a house an' some work sometime . . .

JAIMIE:
She's with me now, David Joe.

RITA: *very torn*
I don't know . . .

JAIMIE:
You don't have to go back, Rita Joe.

RITA JOE looks away from her FATHER with humility. The FATHER turns to JAIMIE PAUL.

He stands ancient and heroic.

FATHER:
I live . . . an' I am afraid. Because . . . I have not done everything. When I have done everything . . . know that my children are safe . . . then . . . it will be alright. Not before.

JAIMIE: *to RITA*
You don't have to go. This is an old man now . . . He has nothing to give . . . nothin' to say!

RITA JOE reacts to both men, her conflict deepening.

FATHER: *turning away from JAIMIE PAUL to RITA JOE*
For a long time . . . a very long time . . . she was in my hands . . . like that!

He cups his hands into shape of a bowl.

Sweet . . . tiny . . . lovin' all the time and wanting love . . .

She shakes his head sadly.

JAIMIE: *angrily*
Go tell it to the white men! They're lookin' for Indians that stay proud even when they hurt . . . just so long's they don't ask for their rights!

The FATHER turns slowly, with great dignity, to JAIMIE PAUL. His gestures show JAIMIE PAUL to be wrong, the old man's spirit was never broken. JAIMIE PAUL understands and looks away.

FATHER:
You're a good boy, Jaimie Paul . . . A good boy . . .

To RITA JOE, talking slowly, painfully.

113

I once seen a dragonfly breakin' its shell to get its wings
. . . It floated on water an' crawled up on a log where
I was sitting . . . It dug its feet into the log an' then it
pulled until the shell bust over its neck. Then it pulled
some more . . . an' slowly its wings slipped out of the
shell . . . like that!

*He shows with his hands how the dragonfly got
his freedom.*

JAIMIE: *angered and deeply moved by the FATHER*
Where you gonna be when they start bustin' our heads
open an' throwing us into jails right across the goddamned country?

FATHER:
Such wings I never seen before . . . folded like an
accordion so fine, like thin glass an' white in the
morning sun . . .

JAIMIE:
We're gonna have to fight to win . . . there's no other
way! They're not listenin' to you, old man! Or to me.

FATHER:
It spread its wings . . . so slowly . . . an' then the wings
opened an' began to flutter . . . Just like that . . . see!
Hesitant at first . . . then stronger . . . an' then the
wings beatin' like that made the dragonfly's body
quiver until the shell on its back falls off . . .

JAIMIE:
Stop kiddin' yourself! We're gonna say no pretty soon
to all the crap that makes us soft an' easy to push this
way . . . that way!

FATHER:
. . . An' the dragonfly . . . flew up . . . up . . . up . . .
into the white sun . . . to the green sky . . . to the sun
. . . faster an' faster . . . Higher . . . Higher!

The FATHER reaches up with his hands, releasing the imaginary dragonfly into the sun, his final words torn out of his heart.

RITA JOE springs to her feet and rushes against JAIMIE PAUL, striking at him with her fists.

RITA: *savagely*
For Chris' sakes, I'm not goin' back! . . . Leave him alone . . . He's everything we got left now!

JAIMIE PAUL stands, frozen by his emotion which he can barely control. The FATHER turns. RITA JOE goes to him.

The FATHER speaks privately to RITA JOE in Indian dialect. They embrace.

He pauses for a long moment to embrace and forgive her everything. Then he goes slowly offstage into the wings of stage left without looking back.

FATHER:
Goodbye, Rita Joe . . . Goodbye, Jaimie Paul . . .

RITA:
Goodbye, Father.

JAIMIE PAUL watches RITA JOE who moves away from him to the front of the stage.

JAIMIE: *to her*
You comin'?

She shakes her head to indicate no, she is staying.

Suddenly JAIMIE PAUL runs away from her diagonally across to the wings of rear stage left. As he nears the wings, the four YOUNG INDIAN MEN emerge, happily on their way to a party.

115

They stop him at his approach. He runs into them, directing them back, his voice breaking with feelings of love and hatred intermingling.

Shouting at them.

Next time . . . in a beer parlour or any place like that . . . I'll go myself or you guys take me home . . . No more white buggers pushin' us out the door or he gets this!

He raises his fist.

The group of YOUNG INDIAN MEN, elated by their newly-found determination, surround JAIMIE PAUL and exit into the wings of the stage. The light dies in back and at stage left.

The MAGISTRATE enters.

There is a light on RITA JOE where she stands. There is also a light around the MAGISTRATE. The MAGISTRATE's voice and purpose are leaden. He has given up on RITA JOE. He is merely performing the formality of condemning her and dismissing her from his conscience.

MAGISTRATE:
I sentence you to thirty days in prison.

RITA: *angry, defiant*
Sure, sure . . . Anything else you know?

MAGISTRATE:
I sentence you to thirty days in prison, with a recommendation you be examined medically and given all necessary treatment at the prison clinic. There is nothing . . . there is nothing I can do now.

RITA: *stoically*
Thank you. Is that right? To thank you?

116

MAGISTRATE:

You'll be back . . . always be back . . . growing older, toughter . . . filthier . . . looking more like stone and prison bars . . . the lines in your face will tell everyone who sees you about prison windows and prison food.

RITA:

No child on the road would remember you, mister!

The MAGISTRATE comes down to stand before her. He has the rambling confidence of detached authority.

MAGISTRATE:

What do you expect? We provide schools for you and you won't attend them because they're out of the way and that little extra effort is too much for you! We came up as a civilization having to . . . yes, claw upwards at times . . . There's nothing wrong with that . . . We give you X-ray chest clinics . . .

He turns away from her and goes to the apron of the stage and speaks directly to the audience.

We give them X-ray chest clinics and three-quarters of them won't show up . . . Those that do frequently get medical attention at one of the hospitals . . .

RITA: *interjecting*
My mother died!

He does not hear her.

MAGISTRATE:

But as soon as they're released they forget they're chronically ill and end up on a drinking party and a long walk home through the snow . . . Next thing . . . they're dead!

RITA: *quietly*
Oh, put me in jail an' then let me go.

MAGISTRATE: *turning to her*
>Some of you get jobs . . . There are jobs, good jobs, if you'd only look around a bit . . . and stick with them when you get them. But no . . . you get a job and promise to stay with it and learn, and two weeks later you're gone for three, four days without explanation . . . Your reliability record is ruined and an employer has to regard you as lazy, undependable . . . What do you expect?

RITA:
>I'm not scared of you now, bastard!

MAGISTRATE:
>You have a mind . . . you have a heart. The cities are open to you to come and go as you wish, yet you gravitate to the slums and skid rows and the shantytown fringes. You become a whore, drunkard, user of narcotics . . . At best, dying of illness or malnutrition . . . At worst, kicked or beaten to death by some angry white scum who finds in you something lower than himself to pound his frustrations out on! What's to be done? You Indians seem to be incapable of taking action to help yourselves. Someone must care for you . . . Who? For how long?

RITA:
>You don't know nothin'!

MAGISTRATE:
>I know . . . I know . . . It's a struggle just to stay alive. I know . . . I understand. That struggle is mine, as well as yours, Rita Joe! The jungle of the executive has as many savage teeth ready to go for the throat as the rundown hotel on the waterfront . . . Your days and hours are numbered, Rita Joe . . . I worry for the child I once saw . . . I have already forgotten the woman!

>*He turns away from her and exits into the wings of stage right.*

118

The lights on RITA JOE fade.

*Lights of cold, eerie blue wash the backdrop of
the stage faintly.*

*RITA JOE stands in silhouette for a long
moment.*

*Slowly, ominously, the three MURDERERS
appear on the ramp backstage, one coming from
the wings of stage right; one from the wings of
stage left; and one rising from the back of the
ramp, climbing it. One of the MURDERERS is
whistling a soft nervous noise throughout their
scene onstage.*

*RITA JOE whimpers in fear, and as the MUR-
DERERS loom above her, she runs along the
apron to stage left.*

*Here she bumps into JAIMIE PAUL who enters.
She screams in fear.*

JAIMIE:
Rita Joe!

RITA: *terrorized*
Jaimie! They're comin'. I seen them comin'!

JAIMIE:
Who's coming? What's the matter, Rita Joe?

RITA:
Men I once dreamed about . . . I seen it all happen
once before . . . an' it was like this . . .

*JAIMIE PAUL laughs and pats her shoulders
reassuringly. He takes her hand and tries to lead
her forward to the apron of the stage, but RITA
JOE is dead, her steps wooden.*

119

JAIMIE:

Don't worry . . . I can take care of myself!

A faint light on the two of them.

RITA:

You been in jail now too, Jaimie Paul . . .

JAIMIE:

So what? Guys in jail was saying that they got to put a man behind bars or the judge don't get paid for being in court to make the trial . . . Funny world, eh, Rita Joe?

RITA: *nods*
Funny world.

The light dies on them. They come forward slowly.

JAIMIE:

I got a room with a hot plate . . . We can have a couple of eggs and some tea before we go to the movie.

RITA:

What was it like for you in jail?

JAIMIE:

So so . . .

JAIMIE PAUL motions for RITA JOE to follow him and moves forward from her.

The distant sound of a train approaching is heard.

She is wooden, coming slowly after him.

RITA:

It was different where the women were . . . It's different to be a woman . . . Some women was wild . . . and they shouted they were riding black horses into a fire I couldn't see . . . There was no fire there, Jaimie!

JAIMIE: *turns to her, takes her arm*
Don't worry . . . We're goin' to eat and then see a movie . . . Come on, Rita Joe!

> *She looks back and sees the MURDERERS rise and slowly approach from the gloom. Her speech becomes thick and unsteady as she follows JAIMIE PAUL to the front of the ramp.*

RITA:
One time I couldn't find the street where I had a room to sleep in . . . Forgot my handbag . . . had no money . . . An old man with a dog said hello, but I couldn't say hello back because I was worried an' my mouth was so sticky I couldn't speak to him . . .

JAIMIE:
Are you comin'?

RITA:
When you're tired an' sick, Jaimie, the city starts to dance . . .

JAIMIE: *taking her hand, pulling her gently along*
Come on, Rita Joe.

RITA:
The street lights start rollin' like wheels an' cement walls feel like they was made of blanket cloth . . .

> *The sound of the train is closer now. The lights of its lamps flicker in back of the stage.*

> *RITA JOE turns to face the MURDERERS, one of whom is whistling ominously. She whimpers in fear and presses herself against JAIMIE PAUL.*

121

JAIMIE PAUL turns and sees the MURDERERS hovering near them.

JAIMIE:
> Don't be scared . . . Nothing to be scared of, Rita Joe . . .

> *To the MURDERERS.*

What the hell do you want?

> *One of the MURDERERS laughs. JAIMIE PAUL pushes RITA JOE back behind himself. He moves towards the MURDERERS.*

> *Taunting them.*

You think I can't take care of myself?

> *With deceptive casualness, the MURDERERS approach him. One of them makes a sudden lurch at JAIMIE PAUL as if to draw him into their circle. JAIMIE PAUL anticipates the trap and takes a flying kick at the MURDERER, knocking him down.*

> *They close around JAIMIE PAUL with precision, then attack. JAIMIE PAUL leaps, but is caught mid-air by the other two. They bring him down and put the boots to him.*

> *RITA JOE screams and runs to him. The train sound is loud and immediate now.*

> *One of the MURDERERS has grabbed RITA JOE. The remaining two raise JAIMIE PAUL to his feet and one knees him viciously in the groin. JAIMIE PAUL screams and doubles over.*

*The lights of the train are upon them. The
MURDERERS leap off the ramp leaving JAIMIE
PAUL in the path of the approaching train.*

*JAIMIE PAUL's death cry becomes the sound of
the train horn. As the train sound roars by, the
MURDERERS return to close in around RITA
JOE.*

*One MURDERER springs forward and grabs
RITA JOE. The other two help to hold her, with
nervous fear and lust.*

*RITA JOE breaks free of them and runs to the
front of the stage. The three MURDERERS
come after her, panting hard.*

*They close in on her leisurely now, playing with
her, knowing that they have her trapped.*

Recorded and overlapping voices . . .

CLERK:
> The court calls Rita Joe . . .

MAGISTRATE:
> Who is she? . . . Let her speak for herself . . .

RITA:
> In the summer it was hot, an' flies hummed . . .

TEACHER:
> A book of verse, a melting pot . . .

MAGISTRATE:
> Thirty days!

FATHER:
> Barkin' to beat hell . . . How! How!

JAIMIE: *laughter, defiant, taunting*
> You go to hell!

PRIEST:
> A confession, Rita Joe . . .

> *Over the voices she hears, the MURDERERS attack.*

> *Dragging her down backwards, they pull her legs open and one MURDERER lowers himself on her.*

RITA:
> Jaimie! Jaimie! Jaimie!

> *RITA JOE's head lolls over sideways. The MURDERERS stare at her and pull back slightly.*

MURDERER: *thickly, rising off her twisted, broken body*
> Shit . . . She's dead . . . We hardly touched her.

> *He hesitates for a moment, then runs, joined by second MURDERER.*

SECOND MURDERER:
> Let's get out of here!

> *They run up onto the ramp and watch as the third MURDERER piteously climbs onto the dead RITA JOE.*

> *Sounds of a funeral chant. MOURNERS appear on riser backstage. RITA JOE's FATHER enters from the wings of stage left, chanting an ancient Indian funeral chant, carrying the body of JAIMIE PAUL.*

> *The MURDERER hesitates in his necrophillic rape and then runs away.*

*The YOUNG INDIAN MEN bring the body of
JAIMIE PAUL over the ramp and approach.
The body is placed down on the podium, beside
RITA JOE's.*

*All the Indians, young and old, kneel around the
two bodies. The FATHER continues his death
chant. The PRIEST enters from the wings of
stage right reciting a prayer. The TEACHER,
SINGER, POLICEMAN and MURDERERS
come with him forming the outside perimeter
around the Indian funeral.*

PRIEST:

Hail Mary, Mother of God . . . Pray for us sinners now
and at the hour of our death . . .

*Repeated until finally EILEEN JOE slowly
rises to her feet and turning to the PRIEST
and WHITE MOURNERS, says softly . . .*

EILEEN: *over the sounds of chanting and praying*
No! . . . No! . . . No more!

*The YOUNG INDIAN MEN rise one after
another facing the outer circle defiantly and
the CAST freezes on stage, except for the
SINGER.*

SINGER:

Oh, the singing bird
Has found its wings
And it's soaring!

My God, what a sight!
On the cold fresh wind of morning! . . .

*During the song, EILEEN JOE steps forward to
the audience and as the song ends, says . . .*

EILEEN:
> When Rita Joe first come to the city, she told me . . .
> The cement made her feet hurt.